MOM! I WANT TO BE A STAR

MOM! I WANT TO BE A STAR

Irene Dreayer

All rights reserved, including without limitation the right to reproduce this book or any portion thereof in any form or by any means, whether electronic or mechanical, now known or hereinafter invented, without the express written permission of the publisher.

Copyright © 2014 by Irene Dreayer

ISBN 978-1-4976-6990-1

This edition published in 2014 by Open Road Integrated Media, Inc.
345 Hudson Street
New York, NY 10014
www.openroadmedia.com

HOW TO USE THIS BOOK

So your child wants to be famous? Who doesn't! If you bought this book then most likely your kid has said to you, "Mom, I want to be a star!" If your child has expressed a desire to be in show business, don't panic. I am here to guide and inform you and your child as to what it takes to go down this path. A career in show business or any business takes extremely hard work and 100% commitment.

As a 30 year veteran of discovering kid stars and producing hit TV shows such as Disney Channel's "The Suite Life on Deck", "The Suite Life of Zack and Cody" and several TV movies, I have seen hundreds of kids try to make it in show business. Most parents and kids don't understand the steps or how to navigate the ins and outs of the industry. Most make critical mistakes unless they are under my management! As Hollywood's only trusted career coach for kid talent, I developed THE DRAY WAY www.thedrayway.com as my method for guiding showbiz kids and their parents. The Dray Way is my method for working with kids and training parents on how to pursue this business we call show in a strategic manner, the right way.

I can't tell you how many times kids tell me on Skype, Facebook & Twitter that they want to be famous. My question to them and to their parents is WHY and WHOSE DREAM IS THIS? There are many unknowns when starting on this adventure, such as how do you know if your kid has talent? Are looks really important? What experience is required? How serious is your child about acting, singing or dancing? How serious are you as parents about helping your child pursue this career? Do you need to move the entire family to LA? What training does your child need? How does this business work? What is your role as the parent? What are the chances your child will get the job? Plus, how do you know if your kid even has what it takes... the "IT" factor?

If you are asking yourself these questions, then this book is required reading. It is a step-by-step instructional guide to read and learn with your child. At the same time, it's fun, humorous, entertaining and filled with personal stories about some of your favorite stars. I feel every parent that has a talented child should know the realities, the inside scoop about show business. I've seen too many parents and their children make the same mistakes over and over again. I wrote this book to give you the real deal, coming from me, about what it takes for your child to explore acting and show business the *right* way, The Dray Way.

The book is designed as a workbook for parents and kids to do together. Every chapter explains, informs and delivers the honest truth about specific aspects of the entertainment business and outlines the crucial information you need to learn, as a family. Some chapters are designed exclusively for parents, but most are a family affair. The exercises in each chapter are to be completed by parents and kids in order to learn the skills required to be a better actor, singer or dancer. Since the book is intended as a step-by-step process, make sure you understand the information and complete the exercises before continuing to the next chapter.

After you have read this book and completed *all* the exercises, you will be educated and have a clearer understanding of the correct steps and necessary skills required to pursue your child's dream.

"Mom! I Want to Be a Star" is entertaining, fun to read and a wonderful opportunity to explore together your child's dream and desire of becoming a star!

So enjoy The Dray Way!

CONTENTS

1. Is Becoming a Star Your Dream or Your Parents' Dream? — 1
2. L.A. Is Not Where You Start; It's Where You End Up — 9
3. Parents, You Are the CEO — 15
4. Parents, Don't Be a Nightmare — 21
5. Parents, Run from Scams — 27
6. Rejection - Let's Rename It — 33
7. It's Not How You Look But How You Feel You Look — 39
8. Keep Yourself Focused When Acting — 45
9. Show Fear the Door — 51
10. Memorizing Is Not Acting; Are You Believable? — 57
11. Bigger & Louder Do Not Make You a Better Actor — 63
12. Act Don't Point — 69
13. Ya Gotta Speak Clearly — 73
14. Can You Find the Joke? — 79
15. Don't Make Excuses for a Bad Performance — 87
16. 14 Should Look 14 — 91
17. I'd Rather Have a Slow 'Yes' Than a Fast 'No' — 97
18. Easy to Get In the Door, Harder to Get Back In — 101
19. Success Is Not Permanent — 105
20. Final Thoughts From the Dray — 111
21. GLOSSARY - Definitions of Industry Terms & Lingo — 113

1
IS BECOMING A STAR YOUR DREAM OR YOUR PARENTS' DREAM?

Act 1, Scene 1, Fade in, open on a young child sitting on a bench ready to begin his or her first scene. The director, a.k.a. "The Dray", yells, "CUT! STOP! Before we start, I need to know: WHOSE DREAM IS THIS?"

Kids, if becoming a star is something you really want, then this book will help you in making your dream come true. If this is your parents' dream for you, then you need to speak up and tell your parents your feelings NOW. In one of my Skype sessions, a mom, sitting next to her daughter, told me that she wanted the same career path for her daughter as Meryl Streep. Mom began by saying, "I want her to be engrossed in every acting class possible; I want her to start with drama because I think that is what she should be doing; I want her to get to the finish line with all the Oscar nominations and wins like Meryl." I then asked the daughter if this was what she wanted. The daughter replied, "I don't know if I want to do this for the rest of my life. I enjoy doing it now because it is fun!" The mom's dreams for her daughter were crushed. The mom then leaned closer and said in a whisper, "I want to Skype with you personally because I want to be an actress too!" Really??? Duh! Ya think? I saw that one coming!

If you are certain that becoming a star is **not your dream**, then close the book and go walk the dog. If you can honestly say that mom and dad aren't making you do this, then keep reading.

I've worked with many kids and their parents and sometimes, the parents' dream for their child is for them to enter the show business world. Do your parents want you to become a doctor, lawyer, teacher or work in the family business, and you want to become a singer, dancer or actor? The same happened with Jennifer Lopez. Her mom wanted her to be a lawyer, but Jennifer had her heart set on becoming a singer and a dancer. If she had followed her mom's dream, where would JLo be now? Not an "American Idol" judge, a recording artist or a movie star! She followed her dream, not her mom's.

You might not know with 100% certainty at your age, that being an entertainer is what you want as a career. Bradley, a young future star I met during an in-person coaching session, had a father and grandfather who were both doctors. The parents assumed that their son would follow the same path. Bradley began studying to become a doctor, and he realized this was not his dream. He left medical school and said to his parents, "I've got to dance!" Currently he is working with a dance group he created called "The Groovaloos" www.groovaloo.com that perform all over the country.

Let's assume you are not in a similar situation as Jennifer and Bradley, and you have your heart set on being a star along with the support of your parents. First, you have to identify what your dream is. Do you want to be a singer, dancer, actor, musician, director, producer, writer, stand-up comic or work behind the camera? Whether it is in show business or as a doctor, lawyer, teacher or fireman, you need to work diligently at your craft in order to make your dreams come true. Are you willing to do the work? And don't say yes if you don't mean it, because you will find yourself in situations out of your comfort zone. You need to devote time to explore anything possible to help you fulfill your dream. Be prepared to work and get to that finish line!

As you watch one of your favorite shows on TV, do you say, "Not only can I do that, but I really <u>want</u> to do that... and I can do it better?" Then, you must work on practicing your craft as much as you can and anywhere you can, such as school and church performances, Community Theater, karaoke, parades, carnivals, group lessons, improv classes... anything that gives you practice and experience.

Mom, Dad, your child cannot pursue their dream without your help and approval. Are you ready to gas up the car, put on your "taxi driver" hat and open your wallet?

The experience and desire is important and necessary, but you need more than that, you need a solid foundation. I always tell kids, "You can't build on wet sand." Translation: To get closer to your dream, you must have a solid foundation along with the talent, the desire, the devotion, the training and the experience. You are going to school and taking classes in math, language arts, history and science to give you a foundation in life. To enter "the school of show business", you must also continue taking classes, no moaning allowed!

Mom, Dad, your child will need your assistance and support in signing up for the right classes, and you will have to manage the schedule between school, training and performances. Your child's dream requires a family effort.

Today's stars require working in all disciplines: singing, dancing and acting. Singers need to take, not only vocal lessons, but also dance classes even if you have two left feet. This increases your lung capacity to give you stamina to hit those high notes like Beyonce and also teaches you how to move naturally like Justin Bieber and Dalton Cyr. Dalton, singer-songwriter, is a Dray Kid winner who took some private dance classes in L.A. with Kanec, a dancer for Justin Bieber, Usher and Chris Brown. Check out Dalton's moves!

Dalton Cyr original song Always

http://youtu.be/bLslV1KJ2b0

Acting classes are just as important for all singers in order to connect with your audience and to portray the emotion of the song. And in a video, you know, we all can see you! Practice writing your own songs to create a catalogue of original material. Songwriting develops your voice and your point of view as an artist. Learn how to read music. Pick up an instrument like a guitar, piano, cello, harmonica, bongos or the didgeridoo www.en.wikipedia.org/wiki/Didgeridoo and continue voice lessons.

Dancers need to take a variety of different styles of dance classes: hip-hop, jazz, contemporary, ballroom, ballet or tap in order to be diversified. Dancers find more opportunities when they are capable of performing any dance. I dreamed of being a dancer myself when I first came to L.A. I auditioned once for a TV special. But, oy, I was way out of my league because I wasn't as prepared as I needed to be. I then realized, "You teach what you need to learn." Acting classes are also vital in the dancer's world. You need to know how to enhance your emotions when dancing... just watch Melanie and Sasha from the popular show "So You Think You Can Dance." www.fox.com/dance/bios/contestants/melanie-moore

Actors should also enroll in diverse acting classes such as: scene study, cold reading, commercial, comedy, drama, voice-over, theater and improv. I also took acting classes, and I learned so much, which contributed tremendously to my work as an Executive Producer and coaching kids. There are as many kinds of acting classes, as there are different kinds of roles. Actors should take singing lessons. It helps your ability to control your breathing and to give you lung power when delivering a big passionate speech as well as a joke with a big punch line. But, you are not done yet. Actors should also take dance classes in order to learn how to move naturally. You definitely don't want to stand there with your hands in your pockets nor do you want to look like you are playing charades as you say the lines.

If stand-up comedy is your dream, write your own jokes that are based on your personal life experiences. There is a lot of funny in truth. The most successful TV, movie and stand-up comedians base their material on life experiences that happen to them. The funniest things you can write about come from your friends, your school, your family, your relatives and even your crazy dog. This is how audiences connect with you and if your stories are funny, you'll have them ROTF and LMHO! A funny thing happened on the way to middle school…

I know, from discovering stars on the Disney Channel, that everyone is looking for that "triple threat," a performer who can sing, dance and act. But, there is nothing wrong with excelling in just one area. You need to identify what you do best because it's better to be good at one thing than mediocre at three. And finally, you don't have to be great at that one thing, you just need to be good ALL THE TIME! And dream big, but make sure it's your dream!

Mom, Dad, it's now your turn to answer: Is this your dream for your child to be a star? Are you pushing your child to be what you want them to be? Can you look at yourself in the mirror with complete honesty and say, "This is not MY dream?"

"Mirror, mirror on the wall, whose dream is it after all?" Maybe you are hesitating to answer. Maybe you are not absolutely sure. Maybe you just don't want to admit it. Read about other parents I have dealt with and their situations. Complete the exercise in this chapter to help you realize whose dream it actually is.

When I begin a Skype session with someone new, the mom or dad or both are always there for this first session. We, of course, introduce ourselves and then I ask my initial question to the child, "Is this your dream or your parents' dream?"

During one of my Skype sessions, every time I asked the girl a question, her Mom answered. She didn't give her daughter an opportunity to answer herself, regardless of the question. When I asked the girl, "Are you taking any acting or music classes?" Mom answered. "How long have you been singing?" Mom answered. "Whose music do you listen to?" Mom answered. "Do you write your own music?" Mom answered. "Are you more comfortable with drama or comedy?" Mom answered. When Mom never let her child speak or answer questions, it was evident that this dream belonged to Mom. Mom was so anxious and in such a hurry to fulfill her <u>own</u> dream for her daughter that she never allowed her daughter to dream for herself. The red light went on! I told the mom, "Stop! I need to hear your daughter answer. Whose dream is this? Yours or your daughter's?" Mom finally stepped aside, and I started all over again asking the daughter the questions without mom's interference.

It's not always Moms. I've seen Dads also answer the questions for their son or daughter. A 9-year-old girl had an in-person session with her Mom and Dad seated behind me. Facing the girl, I began to ask her my questions. The daughter was attempting to speak and began to open her mouth when, from behind me came the answers. It seemed like the dad was the ventriloquist and his daughter was his puppet. At first, this cracked me up, since it seemed that this father-daughter performance was rehearsed. But then, I politely told the dad, "If you don't stop answering for your daughter, I'll have to ask you to wait outside." Dad was quiet and for the first time, his daughter had a big smile on her face!

Mom, Dad, kids... I'm glad you are still reading and now I have a couple of assignments for you. Grab a pencil and paper... you too Dad... and let's do our homework.

Please watch these Drayism videos before proceeding to the exercises in this chapter:

Drayisms by The Dray - Is It My Dream or My Parents Dream?

http://youtu.be/Wdnk1WBVrgg

Drayisms by The Dray - Don't Dream of Success, Work Hard At It

http://youtu.be/37qmFKReyQM

Exercise #1

Kids, make a list of 10 things YOU want to do in your life; what you want to accomplish with your education, your career, your family or your lifelong dreams. Then, have your parents make a list of 10 things THEY want YOU to do in your life. You can have them create this list together or have Mom and dad each make a separate list without conferring with each other. Go in separate rooms so nobody peeks at the others' answers! Now, compare and discuss your list with your parents' list. Find the similarities and differences between what they dream for you and what your own dreams are.

How did you do? If you all still have that common dream, then the next exercise is for the kids… although you might need Mom and Dad to help you remember the agony and defeat of learning some of these skills!

Exercise #2

If this is YOUR dream kids, are you ready to work to make your dream a success? Are you prepared to put forth the repeated effort it takes to successfully perform a song, dance, monologue or musical piece? How many times do you need to practice for that one performance? The same is true for any skill in your life.

Write down approximately how many times you had to work at the following skills in order to master each one? Was it once, two times, 3, 4, 5 or more?

SKILL
Tie your shoe
Do a somersault
Master the hula-hoop
Ride a bike
Ride a skateboard
Type without looking
Dive into a pool
Shoot a free throw
Memorize a monologue
Memorize a song
Learn a dance

PRACTICE, PRACTICE, PRACTICE!! Whether it's a complicated gymnastic trick, a dance routine, a song or a monologue, if it is your dream, you must work at it repeatedly to achieve success.

Dwight Howard, star center on the Orlando Magic basketball team, guest-starred on "The Suite Life on Deck." All his life he dreamed of being a great basketball player, and he achieved that dream by constantly practicing his sport. Dwight had another long-time dream of becoming an actor and is successfully pursuing that dream today. http://thedrayway.com/blog/2011/07/actings-connection-to-sports-dwight-howard-says-its-practice/

So, let's continue pursuing your dream. Think of me as your team coach! We'll discuss strategies, read game plans, have practices and do exercises to score big, win the game and bring home that "Most Valuable Player" award!

All our dreams can come true,
if we have the courage to pursue them.
- Walt Disney

2
L.A. IS NOT WHERE YOU START; IT'S WHERE YOU END UP

If tennis is your game, you wouldn't go to Wimbledon as your first competition. If you are a basketball player, your first game wouldn't be up against Kobe Bryant. If you want to be a world-famous chef, your first attempt in the kitchen would not be against Wolfgang Puck. When you first come to Hollywood, you cannot expect to land a leading role with George Clooney in a major motion picture as your first job.

Before you even consider packing your suntan lotion and coming to L.A., it is imperative that you have exhausted all the resources available to you in your home town. You have taken classes in all areas of acting, singing and dancing at the highest level available to you. You have performed at multiple venues throughout your surrounding area. You have outgrown what your current agents and managers can do for you. Now, you are ready to go to the next level. Hollywood here you come!

I hear all the time, "My daughter performs for friends and family in our living room. They say she is fabulous and should be in show business." Mom, being fabulous in front of 20 people in your living room is not the same as performing in front of 20 million people in their living rooms. A standing ovation by your family of your child's rendition of "Tomorrow" from "Annie" does not mean you are ready to be in show business. It's very different when you audition in front of casting directors and producers than performing in front of grandma and grandpa shouting, "She's a star!"

Kids, first of all, it has to be your dream, and your dream only. Trust me, there's more to being a star than just dreaming about it. You have to be fully prepared and immerse yourself in everything that is needed to make that happen. You need to be on a stage, any stage, such as school plays, community theater, your church, your synagogue or any opportunity where you can perform in front of an audience. Competition can be fierce. As mentioned in chapter one, in addition to acting lessons, you should also take singing and dancing lessons, even though your dream is just to be an actor. Singing and dancing lessons improve an actor's breathing, voice control, stamina and movement on stage. Don't come to L.A. to take your first class. Remember, get your feet wet at home before your try the high dive in Hollywood!

When you are planning to go to college, it is the same approach. You spend your entire school years preparing for college. How do you do that? You choose the best schools, the most challenging classes, varied extra-curricular activities, and you work hard to get the best grades to be accepted into the college of your choice. So, use this approach of preparation and training as if you were planning to attend the "University of Hollywood!"

Mom, Dad, are you prepared? Are you ready to change your entire life? Do you realize this will affect everyone emotionally, financially, logistically and psychologically. There are decisions to be made that affect the entire family. You need to decide on living arrangements before you get off the plane. Research what would be the most feasible housing, both financially and emotionally. You could rent an apartment or house, furnished or unfurnished, mooch on friends or relatives or drive your motor home to L.A. If you have a job that you can do anywhere, that's a plus. Another option that many consider is for one parent and their child to come to L.A., while the rest of the family remains home. You need to have a family meeting to communicate and discuss what this move would mean emotionally for your child. This will mean leaving their friends, brothers or sisters, schoolmates, teachers, pets and the parent who stayed home. Parents, it is your responsibility to insure they are OK with this. This decision involves everyone, so make certain the entire family is on board.

When Jaden Smith did an episode of "The Suite Life of Zack and Cody," his mom and dad (Jada Pinkett and Will Smith) told me that any decisions pertaining to their children's career, Jaden and his sister Willow, are discussed at their family meetings. http://thedrayway.com/blog/2011/06/jaden-smith-the-suite-life-of-zack-and-cody/

I met a 15-year-old boy at one of my speaking engagements at the Oakwood Apartments who had been living in L.A. for 5 years. (Oakwood Apartments is a very well-known complex, where many kids seeking fame and their families stay once they arrive in L.A.) During those 5 years, he was not able to secure an agent or a manager and had never worked. At that time, his grandmother was staying with him, replacing mom and dad who had been taking turns back and forth all those years. He booked a session and auditioned for me. Sadly, I understood why he had no job or representation. He was not ready to be in L.A.! He could have used those five years perfecting his craft in his home town instead of wasting them in L.A. I said to the grandmother, "Go home!" She cried out of relief as their finances were dwindling. Parents, do not make a premature move. If something is not working, send it back!

Parents, do not rent the U-Haul, pack up all your belongings, sell your house, quit your job, withdraw your kids from school, come to L.A. and then meet me. You are doing it backwards. I met a family who was ready to do just that. Luckily, they came to L.A. first to visit and to meet with me and to inform me of their plan for their daughter. The daughter had the desire to pursue a career in show business, but she was nowhere near ready to come to Hollywood. She had no acting or audition experience, not even a school play or community theater audition. These parents were ready to buy the dream for their child. I told them to stop, slow down, back up a bit and take a look at the big picture. It is extremely expensive in L.A., and their daughter is not ready to realize that dream. My suggestion to them was to go back home, unpack, return the trailer, get their jobs back, put their kids back in school and return to L.A. when their daughter had more experience.

When you think your child is ready, make a trip to visit L.A. prior to the big move. This is to get the lay of the land, to line-up classes, set-up agent and manager meetings, investigate housing and find the best opportunities to showcase your child. You don't want to make the move without a plan. The best time for the big move is during pilot season (when they are casting new shows) which is the first part of the year, February to May and October. From July through the fall, new shows start production, and you want to be available for guest starring roles.

Debby Ryan and her family followed the Dray Way. Debby knew this was her dream. She first gained experience in her hometown in Texas before making the trip to L.A. by taking acting, singing and dancing classes, learning how to audition and then began performing locally, including "Barney." As a result, Debby signed with a talent agent in her hometown. That was the best decision she and her family made. Her agent informed her of the audition with the Disney Channel for the starring role of Bailey on "The Suite Life on Deck." Her agent sent in her audition video, and you can guess what happened! She was asked to come to L.A. to audition for the casting directors, producers and cast. Debby Ryan became our Bailey. When she finally signed on the dotted line, she and her family moved to L.A.! And now Debby stars in her own Disney Channel series "Jessie." That's the way to end up in L.A.!

When you are ready to make the big move, I will welcome you to Hollywood with open arms!

Please watch this Drayism video before proceeding to the exercises in this chapter:

Drayisms by the Dray - L.A. Is Not Where You Start!

http://youtu.be/Oj8dBHa-i7g

Exercise #1 - The Family Meeting - Choose any or all of the following guidelines:

- Plan a family meeting when all members are able to gather around the table and discuss the potential move to L.A.
- Each person is entitled to speak freely and have their own opinion.
- Respect each other by allowing each family member to express their feelings and concerns.
- Mom or Dad, it's up to you to hear from everyone, without any one person monopolizing the conversation.
- Every person gives a positive remark about each family member.
- Everyone mentions what their dreams are and how to attain them.
- How would you feel about leaving home and moving to L.A.?
- How would you feel about going to a new school?
- What would you do if you had to leave your friends? How would you maintain your friendships?
- How would you feel if one parent went to live in L.A. with the "future star?"
- What would be the worst part about moving to L.A. or having the family split?

- What would be the best thing about moving to L.A.?
- What are you most scared of regarding this decision?
- Is there anything else that is on your mind?

Exercise # 2

Check-off the items you, your child and your family have completed before your flight to Los Angeles.

Parents' Checklist:

_____ My child has assured us that this is definitely his/her dream.

_____ We have discussed the finances and figured out what we can afford.

_____ We have looked into housing and secured a place to live.

_____ We have made a schedule of which parent will be at home and which will come with our child.

_____ We have researched which acting, singing or dancing classes are the best.

_____ We have researched the best coaches to work with our child one on one.

_____ We have decided on the best public or private school, or have made the choice to homeschool our child.

_____ If we are enrolling our child in school, we have transcripts and all the necessary paperwork.

_____ If we decided on home school, we have all the information and necessary materials.

_____ We have exhausted every resource locally: classes, coaches and performances.

_____ We have read all the chapters in this book and completed all the exercises.

Child's Checklist:

_____ My dream is to be in show business.

_____ I am willing to work to achieve fame.

_____ I have taken many types of acting, singing and dancing classes.

_____ I learned so much in my classes and will apply everything to my performances.

_____ I love all my classes.

_____ I have worked hard in all my classes.

_____ I practiced every day.

_____ I have performed at many events in my community.
_____ I have read all the chapters in this book and completed all the exercises.

Exercise #3

Your parents are doing a lot of research to help you with your dream. Here is an assignment for you to help navigate once you get to L.A.

Go to MapQuest and locate the following areas of town and places you will most likely go. This will help you and your parents determine what area would be the best place to live. You can't be late to an audition or meeting, so it's important to know where you are going. Locate each of the following areas, studios and TV networks and then press PRINT!

Areas	Studios	Networks
Hollywood	Warner Brothers	ABC
West Hollywood	Disney Studios	CBS
North Hollywood	Paramount	NBC
Studio City	Sony	FOX
Sherman Oaks	20th Century Fox	CW
Burbank	Disney Channel	
Culver City		Nickelodeon
Santa Monica		
Venice		
Downtown L.A.		

One more thing! MapQuest the best pizza, ice cream and frozen yogurt places in town to celebrate your arrival in L.A.

Just because you are in Hollywood doesn't mean it will happen.
-Irene Dreayer

If you're not prepared, the only thing you will gain by coming to Hollywood is 3 hours!
-Irene Dreayer

3
PARENTS, YOU ARE THE CEO

Welcome to the world of show "business." It really is a business we call "show." Mom, Dad, you are given the title of CEO - Chief Executive Officer of your child's career. Before we begin, let's define that role:

The CEO is the leader and the decision maker that involves high-level decisions about policy and strategy of any company. The CEO advises and motivates employees, authorizes change, and presides over the organization's day-to-day, month-to-month, and year-to-year operations overseeing the product. The product here is your child.

As CEO, you are the CHIEF, the head of the company. As an EXECUTIVE, you are the authoritative figure who will oversee that all plans for the company are performed. As an OFFICER of this company, you have the final decisions.

Parents ask me time and time again, "What is the difference between an agent and a personal manager?" Parents, you are the CEO. Your child is the product, the agent is the salesman and the personal manager is the marketing director. If these three elements don't work side by side, I don't care what business you are in, it won't run smoothly. You have to understand that your child's agent and personal manager work for free until your child gets a job. It may take weeks, months or years. So, you have to choose those leaders of your team to represent your child in the best way. It can be a long haul for everybody.

As CEO, you are responsible to build your team. The agent, who gets 10% commission, is responsible for getting your child a job. They are the salesman, not necessarily 'warm and fuzzy.' They are all about getting the job. Most agents represent several actors that fall into the same category. One agent may have 15 kids that are blonde, the same age and can sing and act. So, when there is a role to be had, many of their clients will end up competing for the role. Your child might be one of them. So when shopping for an agent, ask if they have an overload of kids similar to yours.

On the other hand, a personal manager advises, consults and is considered the marketing director. They have a much bigger overview of your child's career. They should also be the one you can rely on day to day. A good personal manager will not have several clients of the same type, unlike the agent. You want to find a personal manager whose priority is the product, your child. I've seen too many personal managers sign clients just to better their profile. Also, there are those who will sign just about anybody. It's like throwing spaghetti up against the wall hoping one of them will stick.

I was producing a project and held a casting session where we were looking for five young kids. There were about 40 kids auditioning for the roles. All of them were so green and needed so much work in order to ever be hired. Who were these agents and personal managers who had signed all these kids? I was appalled. If their clients were not ready, they had no business sending these unprepared kids out on auditions. I became furious with these agents and personal managers, signing kids in droves and hoping to win the lottery with one of their clients. Make sure the agent and personal manager have the right marketing strategies for your child.

Another question I often hear is, "Do we need a business manager, a publicist, a stylist, bodyguard and a lawyer?" My answer, "No, not until your child is a star of a hit TV show on a network and/or they are the star of a feature film." If you really have the need to spend unnecessary money on any of the above, go to Vegas. The returns will be about the same. Parents, a.k.a. the CEO, the business manager manages money coming in, not projections, but actual income. A publicist is not worth the $3,500 a month just to publicize that your child went to McDonald's on a Tuesday with a boy who left, and she ate their fries alone. The stylist is paid a fortune to go to Target to buy a red jacket to go with the red shoes. Mom, Dad, save your money and check in the back of your closet first. Vintage is in! Check in the back of Grandma's closet too! And unless you stole the jacket from Target, you don't need a lawyer.

As CEO of your child's company, and also Mom and Dad, it is your job and responsibility to ask the necessary and important questions in advance of an audition:

- What is the audition for?
- What is the rating (of the movie, TV show)?
- What should they wear?
- Is there a script that they need to read?
- Are their lines for them to learn?
- Is this a local shoot?
- What does this job pay?
- Is this a union job? (SAG-AFTRA)
- Do they need to bring their resumé and headshot?
- May I be in the room during the audition?

I had been working with two sisters, who were aspiring actresses, whose parents did not ask these pertinent questions. I got a call from their Dad who drove his daughters into town for an audition at 11:00am on a Sunday. He wanted me to coach them before the audition. I asked Dad and the girls, "What is the audition for? A pilot? A movie? A commercial?" Neither the father nor the girls had a clue what the audition was for. So, we called Mom, who was at home, waiting the results with the rest of the family. I asked her the same questions about the audition, but she did not know either. Wait a minute, it's Sunday at 11:00am in Hollywood! Her 9- and 11-year-old girls were auditioning... for what? Her reply was, "I didn't want to be one of those mothers who kept asking questions." I fell off my chair! I couldn't believe they were going to an audition and did not ask for details except for the time of day and location. Mom, Dad, you are the CEO! It is your job to know.

Many times, I Skype only with the parents to answer their questions and discuss their concerns. I was talking with a Mom about their new manager that signed her child. She did exactly what she was supposed to do... ask him questions. The response she got from her manager was, "Don't call me with all these questions, I'm handling it! Don't worry, everything will be fine." Again, I fell off my chair! The duties of the manager are to provide their client and parents with any and all information that pertains to an audition. The parents brought the manager into the boardroom and said what Donald Trump, CEO, would say, YOU'RE FIRED! Way to go Mom and Dad!

Mom, Dad, you don't want to be in a situation where the agent or manager fires you. Do you call every day, multiple times a day to ask the same questions over and over again, "Will they get a callback? What do you think will happen? Did they like him? What did they say? Do you think they'll get the part? When will we know?" As the CEO, you have hired the representatives that report to you on any and all information regarding your child. Allow them to do their job and when they have an answer, you will know.

Parents, when you are looking at the financial side of this business, you have to be open and understanding. There is an investment side initially, without any guarantees of financial returns, such as headshots, boot camps, acting or dance classes, vocal lessons and coaches. The truth is, this is no different than having your child sign up for the band, cheerleading, football, tennis, golf or other extra-curricular activities. You invest money for uniforms, instruments, training, classes and coaches. There is no guarantee that your son or daughter will be the next Academy Award winning actor just like there is no guarantee that they will be the next Tim Tebow or Serena Williams.

Understand that your child, the product here, should never be regarded as the sole breadwinner of the family. That is not their role.

Please watch this Drayism video before proceeding to the exercises in this chapter:

Drayisms by The Dray - Mom & Dad You Are the CEO!

http://youtu.be/AJ31Zl9KovI

Exercise #1
Read this excellent source of information published by the Screen Actors' Guild. It is a very organized and easy-to-read reference dealing with the business aspects of this industry pertaining to your child. Some of the topics covered are: Union Requirements, SAG Cards, Contracts, Work Permits, Work Day Rules, Education and Financial Responsibilities.

SAG HANDBOOK FOR CHILDREN:
http://youngperformers.sag.org/files/youngperformers/YPH_FNL3.pdf

Exercise #2
Watch the webinars in this chapter:

The Business of the Business Part 1
http://thedrayway.com/webinar-business1.html

The Business of the Business Part 2
http://thedrayway.com/webinar-business2.html

As the chief, the executive and the officer of your business, don't forget you are also the CEO of your family, first and foremost.

Parent is a verb, not who you are.
-Irene Dreayer

Business is a lot like a game of tennis, those who serve well usually end up winning.
-Anonymous

4
PARENTS, DON'T BE A NIGHTMARE

Parents, please don't be a nightmare. It is not something you want to be called. Trust me. Moms who are nightmares, or as we call them, "Stage Mothers from Hell," are more frightening than any bad dream you've ever had. They yell; they bully; they are stubborn, demanding and uncooperative; they can be deceitful, spiteful and inconsiderate of others. The fastest way to prevent your child from ever getting another job is for you to be considered a nightmare.

Nightmare Moms and Nightmare Dads, you know who you are. You are the parents who are screaming and yelling and threatening to behead the coach at your child's soccer game. You are the parents who are ranting and raving about every call that the referee makes. And you are the parents that embarrass your child with your out-of-control, unnecessary and ridiculous behavior. Poor little Billy wants to crawl under the bleachers. A nightmare is a nightmare whether you are on the soccer field, a basketball court or on the stage of Paramount Studios. Your behavior will and does affect whether or not your child will get hired or fired.

During a production week of one of my series, we left the studio to film on location. The cast and crew were required to ride in an insured vehicle with a driver from our production crew. The mom of our young star demanded that her child ride with her in the family car. Because this is against union rules, it potentially could have shut down the production. The union rule requires any stars travelling must be transported by a union vehicle and driver. The mom knew this and chose to disregard policy and was adamant her child ride with her. As a result, we had to hire additional crew ($$$) to travel in front of her car, behind it and next to it for protection. Thank goodness nothing happened. What did happen was that the nightmare had just begun.

Remember parents, you must abide by the rules in order to maintain a good relationship with the network executives, studio and producers. Your child will pay the consequences if you do not behave. It is not your position to demand anything that breaks a rule. Remember kids, you must abide by the rules too.

The nightmare continued with the mom acting as though she was in charge of the production of the show as well as being in charge of casting the show. She did not want us to hire a particular guest star that was to appear on the show. She demanded we not hire them. Excuse me! When did you become Executive Producer? Hello? That would be me! We disregarded her out-of-line behavior, and we hired the guest star, in spite of the mom's protest. So what did mom do? She actually took her child off the show for that week's episode causing the writers to do some creative rewriting. This caused bad rapport between the mom, the network and the entire production crew. Moms, never, ever do anything of this nature. You will lose and more importantly, your child will lose. They will be labeled as, "Oh, you're the one with the crazy nightmare mother!" Who did she think she was? Casting director, writer and producer rolled into one? Mom was a definite nightmare and the network eventually exercised their power and cancelled the show. Not only did her child lose a job, but hundreds of people also lost their jobs.

Parents, do NOT become a nightmare when your kids are auditioning or working on the set. Unless you're an acting coach, don't instruct your child on how they are to read their lines. There are professionals to do that.

I can walk into any audition room or onto any set, and I can pick out which mom belongs to which kid. Each mom is mouthing the words their child is saying, like a bad version of a ventriloquist act. Most of the time, they are unaware that they are even doing this. Mom, first of all, if it is an audition, get out of the room, and if, for whatever reason you're in the room, cover your mouth. The same applies if you are on a set. It's annoying and distracting!

And the nightmares continue...

During rehearsals of the "The Suite Life on Deck," two moms were watching their children perform as guest stars. Every time the kids said their lines, the mothers kept track of the number of lines that each child said. One of the mothers realized that her child had fewer lines. She approached the writers and pitched them an additional line (meaning she gave the writers an idea for an additional line) hoping they would agree. This way, her child would have the same number of lines as the other guest star. She didn't get the line for her child. What she did get was the label… NIGHTMARE!

Mom, you are not alone. Make room for Daddy!

Dad, you too must follow the rules. If you are the guardian on set, you must arrive on time with your child, which is referred to as your call time. That does not mean a quick stop at Starbucks on the way. I've been there, and it's never quick. And if you choose to leave during your lunch or dinner break (highly not recommended), you must be back on time, or better yet, be early. Being late can cost the production company mucho dinero.

One of the dads decided to take his kid, who was hired as a guest star on a TV show, to an audition during a break from filming. The location of the audition was close, and his son was not in the next two scenes, so he decided to take his kid to the audition without letting anyone know they were leaving. Parents, the rule is, you never leave the set with your child until dismissed. It's the same rule for your son on the basketball team. You can't take him out of the game to go get a pizza just because he was sitting on the bench. We ended our break early so we could get ahead of our shooting schedule. Every producer's dream, right? But, the guest star was nowhere to be found, and the dream then turned into a total nightmare. Yes, Dad, I'm talking about you. Dad finally returned our guest star. Were there consequences for the dad's action? Yes, not only was his child embarrassed and humiliated in front of his fellow cast members, but he was never asked to be a part of the show again.

The nightmares are not only limited to the Stage Moms and Dads of the cast, but also those parents who attend a taping with their kids. These parents either went online to get tickets or were invited by a member of our cast or crew. Talk about nightmares! The behavior from some of these parents is astounding.

There was a mom and her daughter who came to a taping of "The Suite Life on Deck", and I realized that I had seen her in the audience at a previous taping. After noticing this woman and her daughter over and over again in the audience, I was curious as to who she was and why she was there every week. I asked my producer's assistant to find out who she was. She went to speak with this woman, came back and said to me, "Dray, she said that she's a good friend of yours!" I had never met this woman in my life. So I went to speak with this so-called friend of mine to apologize for not recognizing her. It turns out she was not and never was a friend. She had used my name each time she called to put her name on the guest list, thereby preventing other kids and their moms from coming to see the show. That is so not fair! I took her aside, and let her know that this was the last time she would be allowed in the audience. Most moms would be embarrassed and ashamed to have been caught using The Dray's name to get into the taping. Oh, no, not this mom. She made a spectacle of herself! She was screaming that her daughter was an amazing actor, and it was imperative that she be discovered and get a role on the show. The young girl wanted to hide as her mom became a nightmare. This is not the type of mom any network would want on their set. There is a right way to introduce your child into this business, and there is a wrong way. The wrong way is yelling and screaming at the Executive Producer and pushing your child upon a producer.

And the nightmares continue...

When parents and their children come to the show, there are no reserved seats for the general public unless you are an invited guest. The families are escorted into the studio and led by the production staff to the audience seating area. A mom and her 7-year-old daughter, who were invited guests, were given two reserved seats in the third row. Oh, but that was just not good enough for this mom. She proceeded to demand (in that extremely loud nightmarish voice) that she absolutely must be in the front row! There was so much commotion that I was called to the scene of the crime! I explained that we seated them in the third row so her very small daughter would be able to see over the railing and over the cameras. That wasn't enough. So, I took the mom and the little girl to the front row and she couldn't see a thing. Duh! Happily, they sat in the third row. The front row is not always the best row.

There are the ultimate nightmares known as "Momagers." You've heard this word! They are moms who think they can handle the management of the career of their child while still being their mom. I have met many mothers of new talent that feel that they can assume the role of Momager. I ask them: Are you able to find the best agent? Do you know which acting classes are right for your child? What vocal coach is best suited for your child? Can you choose the right music producer, choreographer and publicist? Do you know when and how to elevate your child's career, what to do and how to get to the next level? Do you have all the right connections? Can you recognize a scam? Are you able to separate your duties as a mom and Momager? I have witnessed many moms that think they can do both. There are a few celebrities who have had Momagers, and very few have kept them on the payroll or continued a personal relationship with them. See for yourself as I submit Exhibit A into evidence: http://www.latimes.com/entertainment/news/photos/la-et-momagers-pg,0,

Mom, if you can handle all the responsibilities of being Momager while retaining the crown of "Mother of the Year," then, good for you! If not, hire a real talent Manager!

Dina Lohan, mother of Lindsey Lohan, is a classic example of what not to do as the mother of a star. She tried to manage her daughter's career but was more interested in managing her own career... a formula for disaster. I have had a mom, whose child was 11, ask me, "Do you think creating a scandal would increase my daughter's fan base and get her recognized." First, I fell out of my chair, and then I said to her as I would say to all Momagers: HIRE A TALENT MANAGER!

Please watch this Drayism video before proceeding to the exercise in this chapter:

Drayisms by The Dray - Parents, Don't Be a Nightmare!

http://youtu.be/nbYz5IUFqXY

Exercise #1
Parents, repeat each line 10 times:
I will make sure that this is my child's dream and not mine.
I will have my child arrive at the audition or on set on time, if not early.
I will follow the rules set by the network when my child is on the set or in an audition.
I will not yell from the sidelines.
I will not pressure my child by humiliating them in public.
I will refrain from interruption.
I will cooperate with what production decides.
I will give my opinion only when asked.
I will be respectful of other parents' children.
I will avoid being jealous of other parents' children.
I will read a book instead of reading someone the riot act.
I will insure my child is free from scandal.
I will not be a "stage mom" (or "dad").

Kids, if your Mom or Dad resembles anyone in the above stories, please speak up and promise me you will tell them:
MOM, DAD, DON'T BE A NIGHTMARE!
-Irene Dreayer

5
PARENTS, RUN FROM SCAMS!

There are a lot of boot camps, acting classes, dance classes, singing classes and in general a lot of people are offering promises to make your child a star. Once they lure you in, the expenditures never seem to stop, and they really don't care if your son or daughter has any talent at all. They just want you to write the check! Some of these camps and classes offer wonderful, useful information and great training. But, there are many that just want you to spend your money and have no intention of being honest whether your child can act or not. Would you sign up for swimming lessons for your child if the company claimed that their lessons will make your child an Olympic gold medalist? Would you send your child to a golf camp that claimed they would make them the next PGA champion?

During one of my sessions, I met a mom and her 12-year-old son who had travelled all the way from South Africa. Up to that point, mom told me that she had spent $30,000 throughout the United States on various boot camps, acting classes, headshots and travel expenses, hoping for her son to be well on his way to become a star. Most of these boot camps made promises and guaranteed, "We will introduce you to agents, produce your own video, provide professional headshots, offer you all the appropriate classes you need and make your child a star."

I was curious to see if her son had any talent. He should, after $30,000 spent on developing his craft as an actor. OMG, this kid was not good, nor was he talented. And that's putting it mildly! I told the mom that I could have saved her $29,800 because I would have told the truth! This mother was never told that her son didn't have that innate ability as an actor, in other words, he wasn't "wired" to be an actor, and he did not have the "it" factor. They came with 500 colored 8 X 10 headshots; 3 CDs of his music (Oy!); and half a dozen DVD's of his scene performances (Double Oy!!). I felt bad for both the mom and her son. They spent an enormous amount of money for false promises.

I always tell the truth. Sometimes the truth is good, sometimes the truth is bad and sometimes the truth is something parents or kids don't want to hear. I would rather sleep soundly at night than lie to kids and tell them how fantastic they are when they're not. Many of the schools and camps you will encounter don't care. All they want is your money.

Nick Roses, a former talent manager, at Luber Roklin Entertainment, was arrested, charged, fined and given probation in 2011 for operating an advance-fee talent service. What that means is he was asking to be paid to represent kids. He travelled all over the country getting kids to sign up for his summer entertainment industry "boot camps." He would tell parents and kids that if you pay for his boot camps, he will sign your child and guarantee them jobs and a career in exchange for paying the fee for his boot camps. That's illegal folks! You never pay a fee for representation or management.

The Krekorian Talent Scam Prevention Act 0f 2009 (http://www.leginfo.ca.gov/cgi-bin/calawquery?codesection=lab&codebody=&hits=20) specifically forbids talent services from charging money upfront in exchange for the promise of securing employment. It also requires such services post a $50,000 bond with the state of California and necessitates clear language in contracts with aspiring artists. The Screen Actors Guild and the American Federation of Television and Radio Artists were instrumental in passing the Krekorian Act to protect parents and their children from this kind of activity.

Please, go online and read the information at these sites that are designed to help parents and their children in the show business industry. It is extremely important that you find out which classes and which boot camps are legitimate and not a scam.

http://hollywoodmomblog.com/performance-oriented-camps-in-los-angeles-ca/

http://www.bizparentz.org/gettingstarted/avoidingscams.html

Unfortunately, just because it's a law, doesn't mean everybody is going to follow the rules. If that were true, there would be no speeders on the road and everyone would pay their taxes on time. There are still unscrupulous people out there promising you the world if you give them money. So, parents, if an agent or manager wants you to pay before they will sign you... run! If a boot camp promises you success, keep your money. If you come across a boot camp that sounds legit, you still have to be careful that the people working there have your child's best interest at heart. Do your research before signing up for classes or attending any boot camp.

I Skyped with another mom and daughter who lived in Maryland. They had just returned from Florida after her 14-year-old daughter took part in a 3-day acting boot camp. The fee: $7,900! Yikes! The mom told me that during the last day of the workshop, they filmed her daughter pretending that she was acting in a 30-second commercial. The DVD of her performance was the "big deal" everyone got for signing up at the boot camp.

The head of the camp was holding a headshot while she recited this commercial. The mom stood by watching her daughter and noticed that he was holding another girl's headshot. Mom interrupted him while he was giving notes and said, "That picture is not my daughter!" This was not an honest mistake since the two girls did not look anything alike. What a very unprofessional ending after an expensive 3-day weekend!

After hearing the story of their boot camp experience, it was my turn to see the daughter act. They should have asked for a refund. Enough said!

The question is how do you distinguish between a reputable boot camp or acting school and a scam? Look for schools and camps that make NO PROMISES of getting your child an agent or manager, booking auditions, meeting producers and famous show business people or a fabulous career as an actor. These camps and schools should just teach the skills needed for your child to pursue their dream as a performer.

The world is online! But, do not pay anyone that wants to put your child's video online. There are a lot of digital scams now where bloggers promise to write about your kid and post their video. Of course, they want you to pay for this service. DO NOT! They say that they are performance or music critics. Well, critics are journalists and journalists don't ask for money. If you are approached by anyone wanting you to pay for any online service like "Look Books" or "Directory" or "Showcases," DO NOT! The show business industry does not look at them!

There are contests online at a variety of sites like The Dray Way, radio, online networks, tween and teen website, Facebook and YouTube. I encourage you to enter and get as much practice as you can performing. But if they ask you to pay, DO NOT! Blogs about acting and teens are fine, as long as they don't ask for money or "partially clothed" pictures. I'm serious, they are out there, so be careful!

Here's my personal scam story. I met a mom who told me that she heard a commercial on the radio in her home state of Maryland. The commercial was for a boot camp, that if you sign up and pay for this particular boot camp, every kid would have an opportunity to audition for and meet the Executive Producer of "The Suite Life On Deck" and possibly book an appearance on the show. Guess what? We had stopped taping the show 18 months prior to this radio commercial! What? Was I supposed to be in Maryland?

Two words: promise and guarantee. If you ever hear these words... close your checkbook and run!

Watch the following Drayism video before proceeding to the exercises in this chapter:

Drayisms by The Dray - Run! From Scams Parents

http://youtu.be/S6Hnf-T3DQU

Exercises
Parents, here are your homework assignments:
1. Read the Krekorian Talent Scam Prevention Act
   http://www.leginfo.ca.gov/cgi-bin/calawquery?codesection=lab&codebody=&hits=20
   Scroll down to Chapter 4.5 Pages 1700-1705.4
2. Research boot camps and classes before you sign up and pay. There are numerous sites where you can ask about scams and read about other people's experiences. Here is a list for you to check out:
   www.scams.com
   www.snopes.com
   www.ripoffreport.com
   www.starsearchcasting.com (check out the forum section)
   www.yelp.com
   Check with people who have attended or check with me!
3. One site that I recommend you read is www.hollywoodmomblog.com. They are a positive community, forum, news outlet, information resource and occasional laugh for the parents of professional children in the entertainment industry in Hollywood and throughout the world. The following

link will take you to a full listing of camps, classes and coaches: http://hollywoodmomblog.com/performance-oriented-camps-in-los-angeles-ca/
4. Read my blog "Scamming Kids in Hollywood" http://thedrayway.com/blog/2011/04/the-dray-way-scamming-kids-in-hollywood/
5. Read my blog "Acting Workshop Scams" http://thedrayway.com/blog/2011/04/beware-acting-workshop-scams/

Beware of agencies that charge you an upfront fee.
Watch out for kickbacks.
Be wary of too much flattery.
No agency can guarantee work.
Is the agency licensed or registered properly?
Be skeptical of agencies that advertise heavily for new clients.
Legit agencies don't impose time limits or pressure about contracts.
And if it sounds too good to be true… it usually is!

6
REJECTION – LET'S RENAME IT

Rejection, that dirty little word! The fear of rejection is the number one reason that prevents parents from allowing their child to pursue their dream to become a star. They are afraid that their child will not be able to handle all the rejection that comes with being in show business. Rejection isn't just a part of show business; it is a part of life. PARENTS, rejection doesn't stop at 11!

Whether you are in show business or not in show business, you will face rejection throughout your life. I encountered rejection recently, and trust me, I am older than 11! I pitched a movie idea to ABC Family and they said no. Ouch! There's that dirty word! I said to myself, "I'm not taking the rejection personally." So what did I do? I went to another network and they said, "Yes!" I took that ugly word "rejection" and renamed it to "It just wasn't right for them."

As an Executive Producer of kid programming, let me explain the difficulties in casting a role. There are so many factors that affect our decision on who we cast. If you didn't get the job, many times it has nothing to do with how talented you are or whether or not you did a great job in the audition. At times the "rejection" was because you were too tall for the role. Or, even though you were the right age, you looked too young. Sometimes, the network executives change their mind about the character, and they now want an older kid. Or, maybe instead of a boy character, they now want a girl. It's crazy how things can change so fast! So, rejection, rename it: too tall, too short, too young, too old, wrong gender, too blonde, too fat, too thin... and now the role has been changed to a dog!! (Don't laugh, this really happened!)

I produced a pilot (a one-episode TV show that networks test before greenlighting to a series) for the Disney Channel called, "Triple Play." The network did not choose this pilot to be on their fall schedule of new shows, so that's why you've never seen it. We cast an unknown actor as the lead, and this was his first TV role. Because the show was not given the 'green light' to be on the air, this actor felt rejected. I remember saying to him, "The show was rejected, not you. You are going to be a very big star!" And now he is! He went on to star in the fabulous "High School Musical" and its sequels. "Just Keep Ya Head in the Game. U Gotta Get'cha Get'cha Head in the Game." Sorry, I get carried away. And his name is? Drum roll please! ZAC EFRON!

Get'cha Head in the Game - Zac Efron (Troy Bolton)

http://youtu.be/gIX_2Yl786Y

Parents, knowing that the rejection of your child for a specific role may have nothing to do with your kid's abilities, it is up to you to create a more positive experience for your child no matter what happens. So guess what parents, you have the biggest role to play; you have to be better actors than your child! Remember every audition should be a learning experience. Make it fun! If your child gets a NO, they are going to ask you, "Why didn't they pick me? Why didn't they like me? Was I not good enough?" You need to turn that NO into a YES when talking to your child. Tell them, "Yes, you were very good, and they want to see you again. It's just this time, the show needs the character to be completely different, that's all."

On the flip side, after a casting session for "The Suite Life of Zack and Cody," I experienced a situation with a mom who was not able to handle the rejection of her child who did not get the part. Her daughter auditioned for a role on the show, but she was not quite good enough to be cast and was not given a callback. Her "I won't take no for an answer" mom brought her daughter back the next day ignoring the fact that she did not have a callback. Attention all moms: DO NOT DO THIS! REALLY? Mom, go back and read chapter 1: Is this your dream or your daughter's? I might have been the only producer in history that allowed this girl to audition again. I felt bad for the kid, and her audition was no better than the previous day. Mom, never put your child in such an embarrassing situation! You need to handle rejection for yourself so you can manage the rejection for your child.

Parents, make sure what your child is striving for is attainable, no matter what their dream is. If your child loves football and aspires to be the on the football team, but lacks the size and the ability, help them gear their dreams where they could succeed: working with the coaches, sports writer for the school paper, head of the pep club, water boy, or a different sport altogether. Tennis anyone? Maybe your child is not ready to take a lead role but would be fantastic in a smaller role. Don't set your child up for rejection purely because it is your dream. Are you pushing them to be something you want? Remember, it's better to have a small role in a great movie than the lead in a piece-of-crap movie.

Yes, Hollywood is filled with rejection but so is life. Think about all those kids that weren't selected for a sports team, were not part of the popular crowd, did not get asked to the dance, were not chosen as Prom King or Queen, or didn't get into their college of choice. Disappointment, self-doubt, fear, loss of confidence and the feeling of not being good enough are painful! As adults, you also encounter rejection: not getting the job, losing the promotion, unrequited love and or your mortgage re-finance application was rejected. Learning how to deal with rejection as a child is an invaluable lesson in life! You will be more equipped to handle what life hands you, and you will have the skills to rename rejection. This way, you can just keep looking forward and on to the next audition in life!

I discovered a beautiful 12-year-old talented singer, songwriter and actress named Suite Caroline. Ironically, she had added the 'Suite' to her name because her favorite show was "The Suite Life of Zack and Cody." I took Suite Caroline to Disney to audition for a role on a pilot that required singing as well as acting. She was rejected. I knew Caroline was extremely talented. Fortunately, her parents were the best example of how to help their child handle rejection. They reminded her that the role was just not right for her. As a result, I wanted to continue working with her along with her parents. Suite Caroline became a client of one of the largest agencies representing Nashville Country Artists; as well as being signed to the number one country music manager in the business… at 13 years old! The icing on the cake was that Sony Music signed her to their label as an artist as well as a publishing deal. Goodbye rejection! Hello Country Music Awards! www.suitecarolinemusic.com

When I take a talented performer like you or anyone to a network, a studio or a production company, I remind every potential star how fabulous it is that we are here, meeting the people that make all your favorite TV shows or feature films. I make sure they understand how exciting it is just to be in the meeting and to have such a unique opportunity. On the way up in the elevator, I remind them, "Whatever happens in these meetings, remember how special you are to have gotten as far as you have." When you audition for a TV show, feature film, a play or commercial, it should be a fun learning experience. If you get a job, that's great! If not this time, there will be more opportunities as you continue pursuing your dream.

When we were casting for the role of Bailey on "The Suite Life on Deck," the final decision was between two girls. We auditioned both girls with Dylan, Cole and Brenda. The girl we ended up casting for the role is Disney Star, Debby Ryan. She was just a better fit. The other girl, who auditioned but did not get the role, was liked by us producers. Rejection! Let's rename it. We brought her back for a major guest-starring role on the show. When one door closes, another one opens.

Please watch this Drayism video and this Webinar video before proceeding to the exercises in this chapter:

Drayisms by The Dray - Rejection, Let's Rename It

http://youtu.be/K3XQw_QfGVY

Webinar: http://thedrayway.com/webinar-rejection.html

Exercises #1

Parents, here is how to turn the "no" your child received after an audition into a positive "yes." Work on telling your child one or all of the following.

a. "Yes, I heard your audition was excellent, but the show needed someone who was taller, heavier, ethnic or a different gender. Or, they simply wrote out the role.
b. "Yes, that was a fantastic experience and only one of many to come. Let's go get an ice cream sundae!
c. "Yes, you are talented. You only had a 'no' because you are tall for your age, and we just can't change that, but they loved your acting, and yes, they will have you back.
d. If the 'no' was something we can change, then, yes, I will help you work on that.

c. The casting director said no, you were not right for this role, but, yes, they will bring you in again for another role.

Exercise #2
Parents, based on your own child's abilities, talents and outstanding characteristics, make a list of all the "yeses" that you would say to your child.

For example, "You did not get the part this time, but YES…"
You are a great dancer.
You were awesome playing the guitar in the audition.
You knew all your lines.
You were focused.
I love you no matter what!

Exercise #3
Kids, this exercise is for you. Talent comes in all different packages.
   I want you to fill in these blanks as you do when you arrive for an audition:

My hair is _____, _____ and _____.
I am _____ feet and _____ inches tall.
I weigh about _____ pounds.
My body type is _____.
My feet are very _____.
My muscles are _____.
My skin color is _____.
The instrument I play is _____.
My best accent is _____.
I am _____ years old.
I am a _____. (boy or girl)

Let's say you audition for a role, and you don't get the part. You find out that all of these descriptions have nothing to do with your acting ability. You just don't fit the role.

Parents, kids, remember: Rejection! Let's Rename It!

Victoria Justice did! She auditioned for her own show on one network. She got a "no" but she turned it into a "yes" at Nickelodeon. Hello "Victorious!"

http://www.nick.com/shows/victorious

7
IT'S NOT HOW YOU LOOK, BUT HOW YOU FEEL YOU LOOK

How you feel you look says more about who you are than what you look like. So many teens are struggling with who they are by the mere definition of how they look. Feeling good about yourself is the most attractive attribute you could have. If you are confident in exactly who you are as a person, inside and out, looks do not matter. Beauty lies within.

The entertainment business is a business of talent and image. The media constantly bombards us with images of what beauty and perfection should look like. What they don't reveal is that the seemingly perfect bodies and flawless skin is due to airbrushing and photo shopping. So kids, don't compare yourself to celebrity photos in the media. The perfectly shaped thighs, the 6-pack abs on guys and the zit-free skin are not how these actors or models look in real life. Don't think that you have to look JUST LIKE THAT, because they don't even look JUST LIKE THAT.

Jada Pinkett Smith once said on the "Oprah Show" how she grew up feeling extremely insecure about her height (Jada is 4 feet and 11.5 inches). Jada stated, "I just had to learn how to love me. And as long as you love yourself, people have no choice but to accept what you are." By accepting yourself and loving yourself, you will gain the confidence you need to pursue any dream you may have or to reach any goal in life.

Some things you can't change, like your height, and some things you can, like your hair. I'm a big believer in how a different haircut, a new style or color can change your attitude about yourself. If your child resents their frizzy hair because it makes them look like a chia pet http://nothing-but-chia.com/the-original-chia-pet-commercial/, do what I did. I hated my long frizzy brown hair. There was a time when I wanted to shave my head (pre-Britney Spears)! I realized that shaving my hair off was not an option. Because my hair was so damaged, I thought the best thing to do was to cut it all off and start over. People would say to me, "Oh, you must have had a lot of confidence to cut off all your hair." My choice to cut my hair gave me a tremendous amount of confidence in myself. It was bold; it was freeing; it empowered me. I love my new look and would never go back to the way it was… ever! So, sometimes even a simple haircut can help you feel good about yourself, regardless of other people's opinion.

Show off your freckles. Be proud of your larger than normal nose. Like me, I'm proud of mine! All the better to sniff out new talent! I like that I don't look like everybody else. So, love that you are tall or short. Embrace your big bones. These unique traits are a part of your identity but don't solely define who you are. I just might be looking for a short freckled-face girl with a large nose for a role in a movie or TV show! Actors come in every size and shape, petite or tall, muscular or lean. There are roles for every different type of kid… and not just in show business. Most bodyguards are big, tall and muscular. Jockeys need to be very short and lightweight. You don't have to look like Miley, Selena or Taylor Lautner to be a talented actor. Hollywood never knows what type of look makes a star. It's all about the overall package and the "it" factor that makes a star.

Owen Wilson starred in Woody Allen's Oscar-nominated "Midnight in Paris" (http://www.imdb.com/title/tt1605783/). When he was younger, he smashed his nose twice from playing football in high school and with friends. He chose to keep his imperfect nose and has gone on to have an amazing career. Melissa McCarthy, one of the funniest actresses today, was nominated for best supporting actress in the feature film "Bridesmaid" (http://www.imdb.com/title/tt1478338/). She also stars in a hit TV show for CBS, "Mike and Molly" (http://www.imdb.com/title/tt1608180/), where she plays an overweight, beautiful and extremely funny woman. Melissa McCarthy started her own plus-size clothing line. Talk about feeling good about yourself!

Matt Timmons from "The Suite Life on Deck" was cast in the role of Woody, not because he was your typical good-looking "Brad Pitt" kind of guy or because he had a long list of experience. In fact, his list had one prior role. He played a bale of hay in "Robin Hood." But he felt good about himself even though he was a bit overweight, wore braces, had bad skin and curly wild hair. He had personality plus and even considered himself a "babe magnet." He loved what he was doing, and it was evident in his performance. It was his unique look, his confidence and self-assurance as well as talent that landed him the role. http://thedrayway.com/blog/2010/11/matt-timmons-casting-a-kid-with-no-credits/

Some of you may not think you are beautiful on the outside. Says who? What is beauty anyway? The most popular girl in school, who is considered the most beautiful, could also be mean, selfish and rude. What does she see when she looks in the mirror? How does she feel about herself? She may see beauty on the outside but how can she feel beautiful on the inside when she treats others with such cruelty. Mirror, mirror on the wall, who's the fairest of them all? YOU!

Being what you think is beautiful doesn't make you smarter or play a piano better or make you a better actor. Be proud of you! Be happy with your accomplishments! Be confident in everything that makes you an equally beautiful person in many other ways. When you audition for a role, you must have confidence in who you are before you can portray somebody else.

I have read and heard about kids, as young as 8 years old, getting plastic surgery, botox injections or liposuction in order to have a perfect look. Mom, what are you thinking? That is just wrong! Mom, you are setting them up to have less value for how they look now and in the future. What happens at 12? A face lift? http://abcnews.go.com/Health/mom-gave-daughter-botox-investigated/story?id=13595955. If your child is unhappy about their weight, help them feel better about themselves by planning healthier meals and make exercising a family event. Before going to the extreme, there is nothing wrong with a little (and notice I said 'little') age-appropriate bit of makeup to highlight their positive points. If a little makeup, a different hairstyle, new glasses or contacts make you more confident and feel good about yourself, then great! It's all about how you feel you look.

Ashley Tisdale, from "The Suite Life of Zack and Cody" and "High School Musical" was always a beautiful girl, but she did not feel that way. She had long brown curly frizzy hair. I asked her, "Will you trust me?" She did, so I took her to my hairdresser who gave her a fabulous cut and made her a blonde. Ashley then felt great about herself.

When you look in the mirror, what do you see? Someone tall or short? Someone thin or overweight? A blonde or brunette? A redhead with freckles? Straight or tiny nose? Blue or green eyes? Long or short hair? What you don't see when you look in the mirror is that you are a good student, you play an instrument, you have a kind heart and soul, you are generous, you're honest and you love pets. Nor do you see what a fabulous actor, singer or dancer you are. Look again! You can't see all these wonderful attributes you have nor can you see anybody else's. But they are part of who you are. These are the things that should make you feel good about yourself, not only what you see in the mirror. It's not how you look, but how you feel you look that matters.

Please watch this Drayism video before proceeding to the exercises in this chapter:

Drayisms by The Dray - It's Not How You Look But How You Feel You Look

http://youtu.be/kn6tWe6fNK8

Exercise #1
1) Make a list of the things you feel are wrong with you and you want to change.
2) Make a list of the things you actually can change.
3) Make a list of how each of these changes will make a difference in how you feel about yourself and why.

Exercise #2
Make a list of all your outstanding qualities that have nothing to do with your appearance, such as: personality traits, talents, abilities, knowledge and any other characteristics that define you as a person.

Now, have your mom, dad, best friend, boyfriend or girlfriend make the same list about your outstanding qualities. Then, compare. You may find other qualities that you didn't think you had.

Post your combined "outstanding qualities" list on the mirror in your bedroom to remind yourself how fabulous you are.

Exercise #3
Mom, please read this wonderful article, with your daughter, about "Empowering Girls," that occurred on "The Oprah Show." http://www.oprah.com/oprahshow/Empowering-Girls/1

Oprah speaks with celebrities and counselors about teen girls, their sense of value and self affirmation. They discuss the mother's role in helping their daughter feel good and proud about whom she is.

Exercise #4

Before you make any drastic hairstyle or makeup changes, first, see how you would look using this virtual makeover website: http://www.instyle.com/instyle/makeover

Always be a first-rate version of yourself,
instead of a second-rate version of somebody else.
-Anonymous

8
KEEP YOURSELF FOCUSED WHEN ACTING

Parents and kids, it is extremely important for all of you to be focused at an audition. What I mean by that is to not let any outside distractions interfere with a successful audition.

When you first arrive to an audition, you are usually seated in a waiting area. All the other moms, dads and kids are there as well, anxiously waiting for their child's turn to audition. It is human nature to start assessing and comparing your child to the other kids that are there for the same role. As you look around, you notice that there are so many kids of different looks, ages, sizes and ethnicities. You are probably thinking, "Oh no, none of these other kids look like my son! Everyone is either taller or older and there's even a girl reading for the part!" You start shaking in your shoes, breaking out in a sweat and already have begun to feel bad for your child because you've convinced yourself he is not going to get the part. Mom, STOP! Focus just on your own child. Your nerves are extremely contagious. I'm even getting nervous writing this. Stop comparing – it does no good. Many times waiting rooms are filled with a diversity of actors because the producers may not know exactly what they are looking for until it walks into the room.

On the other hand, your child, who is 12, blonde and short, may be auditioning for a role where the requirement is to be 12, blonde and short. And here you are probably thinking, "Oh no. All of these kids look like my son!" Mom, I can see your nervous foot shaking again. STOP! Focus just on your own child – it does no good to compare. The only thing that will happen is your nerves will make your child nervous. Be calm and remember, your only job at this point is to keep your child focused on the material and his audition.

The one and only thing you should focus on at an audition is making sure your child is prepared, relaxed and most importantly confident about themselves. Leave your nerves at home.

Kids, focus on your material and how hard you have worked to get to this point. Then, think about the flavor of ice cream you are going to have once you have finished this audition… and convince your mom to take you, you deserve it!

Mom, how many times have you asked your child a question and the answer you got was, "Huh?" He was not focused! He was not concentrating or listening to what you were saying. Help your child to be focused at home. These same focus skills will benefit your child in school as well as in job training and ultimately in their career. When they are at an audition and they are given a direction, being focused is the key! They have to listen, understand and apply what they are being told to do in a scene.

Kids, an important aspect of focusing is to listen and look directly at the person with whom you are speaking. The same is true if you are at an interview for a job or an important meeting. Look at and listen to the person who is speaking. At an audition, you must look straight into the eyes of whoever is reading the scene with you, even if they are reading many different parts. Eye wandering and darting all over the place is very common amongst inexperienced kids. When casting agents, producers and directors see eye darting; it's a red flag that you are not a focused actor. It's also a red flag that you will not be able to take direction, which is extremely important, or that you will not be able to handle a line change or a scene change on a dime.

One of the Dray Kids I work with used to have a terrible habit of darting his eyes away from the person with whom he was speaking. During Skype sessions, his eyes never focused on me. Instead, he looked up, down, right, left and everywhere else except at the camera. I asked him why he was doing that. His response was, "Doing what?" The first step in solving any focus problem is for the person to be aware that they even have a problem. He had no clue he was darting his eyes all over the place. When he started to read a scene with me, I couldn't follow his eyes – as if they were in a pinball machine. The second step is to understand why you have a lack of focus. Eye darting is an indication of your insecurity in your ability to deliver the lines correctly. In other words, you have a fear of doing it wrong! It's OK to make a choice, even if it is the wrong choice. You need to remain confident. Focus, focus, focus! Then I gave him exercises to help him be focused and finally, we see eye to eye!

Zac Efron, in the beginning of his career, also had an 'eye darting' issue. It was just a matter of beefing up his confidence. And those big blue eyes became very focused. And now he has an extremely focused movie-star career.

Mom, Dad, I need your help in keeping your child focused! Watch your child as they practice their song, monologue or scene at home. Observe them and watch for telltale signs that indicate they have a lack of focus. Watch for the eye darting I spoke about and any other habits. Most kids, and even sometimes adults, only expose their habits when they become nervous.

During one of the Dray Way Skype sessions, a girl had the habit of making a weird facial expression at the end of every sentence, but only when she was acting. I asked her why do you bite your lips at the end of every sentence? She didn't even realize she was doing anything out of the ordinary. I told her to take her laptop "and me" into the bathroom. She placed the laptop on the vanity in front of the mirror. I asked her to do the scene as she looked in the mirror and as I watched her on my screen, She did it exactly as she had done it before, and ended every line "biting her lips." She started crying. I asked her why she was crying and she said, "Nobody ever told me I was doing that." She thanked me for telling her. So, she practiced doing her lines from that day on in the bathroom until she was able to control her nervous habit and be completely focused.

Please watch the Drayism video before proceeding to the exercises in this chapter:

Drayisms by The Dray - Keep Yourself Focused in an Audition

http://youtu.be/YC8FFQpl-bU

Exercise #1
This exercise will help you become aware of any nervous habits, which indicate your lack of focus.

Your turn to go into the bathroom and practice your song or your dialogue lines in front of the mirror. In some cases, you might want to use a full-length mirror.

- Do the lines and watch yourself in the mirror.
- Do you scrunch your face?
- Do you roll your eyeballs?
- Do you lick your lips over and over?
- Do you push your hair behind your ears? (Girls, please put your hair in a ponytail as long as it's out of your face)
- Do you find yourself looking at the shower door instead of yourself?
- Do you rock back and forth?
- Do you look down?
- Do you bounce up and down?
- Do you need a haircut?

Exercise #2
To eye dart or not to eye dart… NOT!

Get 2 regular pieces of paper (8½ x 11) and write about 20 words on each one. Make the words fairly big (so you don't need glasses to read them up close!). Hold one sheet on either side of your face, therefore blocking your peripheral vision. Now, say your lines! If you can see the words you wrote on the papers, your eyes are darting. Focus straight ahead. I know it's not easy, and the temptation is great. But, once you can focus, you will not have an eye darting problem.

Exercise #3
Shoot video of yourself performing in front of people, as much as possible. You should be able to see any bad habits that affect your focus and your performance. Just like the day after a football game when the players watch replays of the game, you be the coach and see what needs to be improved for the next game or your next performance. (But don't yell at yourself too much!)

Exercise #4
Parents, in order for your child to focus before going into an audition, you need to help them relax. They don't need to focus on everyone and everything around the room as you wait. Here are some ideas to help both of you:

Go outside or in the hall to practice (away from others).
Play word games, card games or board games.
Play hangman or tic-tac-toe.

Listen to music on your iphone.
Plan your after-audition celebration meal or menu.

Nerves cause lack of focus.
Lack of focus does not get you a callback!
-Anonymous

9
SHOW FEAR THE DOOR

We all experience fear in different ways. There is the kind of fear you experience when you are sitting in a movie theatre, and you find yourself hiding under the coat of the person next to you watching "Friday the 13th," "Paranormal Activity," "Nightmare on Elm Street" or "Saw." Another type of fear is referred to as *phobias*. Some common ones are insectophobia - fear of bugs, batophobia - fear of heights, scolionophobia - fear of school, spermophobia - fear of germs and testophobia - fear of taking tests. Phobias that are not as common are sesquipedalophobia - fear of long words, telephonophobia - fear of telephones and syngenesophobia - fear of relatives.

You may not be afraid of bugs, scary movies or telephones, but do you suffer from *glossophobia*? This is a persistent, abnormal, and unwarranted fear or physical aversion of public appearance, despite conscious understanding by the phobic individual and reassurance by others that there is no danger. In other words, do you suffer from audition anxiety? (http://www.changethatsrightnow.com/audition-anxiety/)

Many kids as well as adults are afraid of public speaking whether giving an oral book report in 4th grade or speaking at a conference of 2,000 employees. So what do you do if you want to be an actor where you are required to perform in front of people? You have to "Show Fear the Door!" Take that performance anxiety and turn it into performance excitement. What should be going on in your head is, "I get to audition for my favorite show! I am so excited to be here! I am so ready to do a fabulous job!" Before you enter the audition room and your knees are shaking, you are sweating and you're glossophobic, let the character you are auditioning for take over and enter the room. Tell your nervous self to wait outside, you'll be right back!

There are tons of famous celebrities who experience performance panic as opposed to performance excitement. Christina Aguilera forgot the words to the National Anthem during the Super Bowl in front of millions of people.

Christina Aguilera - National Anthem - Superbowl 2011 HD

http://youtu.be/hj5NPNe3jNU.

She forgot to "show fear the door," but when she turns her chair around on "The Voice," http://www.nbc.com/the-voice/ she's fearless! Zac Efron of "High School Musical" fame confessed that he was scared and overwhelmed to play the role of a Marine in "The Lucky One." http://theluckyonemovie.warnerbros.com/index.html# Even though he had limited acting experience and came from a musical theater background, he was able to show fear the door and gave an outstanding dramatic performance. Sofia Vergara was terrified that *Latinas* would be offended by her character on "Modern Family." http://abc.go.com/shows/modern-family But, she turned aspects of her role into a positive by showing intense love and over-protection of her children. Did I just hear the door slam again? I believe that was fear leaving. Derek Jeter, renowned Yankee All-Star said, "I was scared to death" while hosting "Saturday Night Live." http://www.hulu.com/watch/200724/saturday-night-live-derek-jeter When he showed fear the door, he found his comedy experience "enjoyable."

I had a boy come in for an audition for "The Suite Life of Zack and Cody" who was shaking so hard, it looked like he was fanning himself with the sides he was holding. I asked him to read a couple of times, but he couldn't stop trembling. I took him out in the hallway and I said, "Is 'Suite Life' your favorite show?" He said yes. "Are you nervous?" He said yes. I then asked, "Do you want to be on the show?" And of course, he said yes. As we stood outside the casting room door, I said, "Leave your nervous self on this side of the door and walk into the audition as the character... and remember your character is not nervous." He walked back into the audition in character and there was no more shaking!

MOM! I WANT TO BE A STAR

Let's look at some of the reasons that make you nervous and cause fear for an audition:

1) You toss and turn all night, worrying about your audition and not sleeping. You have caused yourself to have low energy and not be on your game.
2) You don't eat all day or the day before an audition. You will become light-headed and unfocused.
3) When you worry about other things outside of the audition, like homework or a big test, you are causing more anxiety and fear for yourself. Also, your focus is not on your audition.
4) If you did not practice your lines enough, you will forget them in your audition. So, make sure you are well-rehearsed.
5) The biggest reason to be nervous is if this is your first audition.

So, you need to sleep, eat, not worry, be prepared and know that the more you audition, the less nervous you will be. This also applies to anything you want to achieve in life. Whether you are interviewing for a job, giving your campaign speech for class president or trying out for cheerleading, show fear the door!

During one of my speaking engagements to a group of moms and kids, a young girl came to the front of the room do a scene with me. After just three sentences into the scene, she fainted and hit the floor in front of everybody. Not only did her nerves get the best of her, she had not eaten all day. Mom, always carry healthy snacks in your purse or in the car. You never know how long a day it can be.

When I was developing the TV show "Sister Sister" for the WB, I helped Tia and Tamera Mowry http://www.mystyle.com/mystyle/shows/tiaandtamera/index.jsp put their audition together. They were nervous and afraid. I remembered what Suzanne dePasse, TV, music and film producer, who discovered Michael Jackson, told me about Michael. He was always nervous before he stepped out on the stage, but the performer side in him made the decision to leave the fear and nerves behind. I told this story to Tia and Tamera, and they were inspired by Michael Jackson. They told me, "If he can do it, we can do it too." And the Mowry twins were able to show fear the door like Michael.

Please watch this Drayism video before proceeding to the next chapter:

Drayisms by the Dray - Show Fear the Door

http://youtu.be/z6jHXrYeWw0

Exercise #1
Here are some things you can do to calm those nerves the day of your audition or performance right before you go in the door:

- Psych yourself up – confidence combats stress
- Visualize a successful audition or performance
- Do breathing exercises
- Run around the block; ride your bike; shoot some hoops
- Stretch
- Do some vocal warm-ups
- Do something silly
- Think positive
- Chew gum (but spit it out before your performance!!)
- Listen to music on your iPhone
- Pray (if you are religious)
- Bring your good luck charm like Cameron Diaz and Brad Pitt who have special necklaces
- And don't forget to practice!

Exercise #2
Use your imagination and before you go into the audition room, choose 2 of your favorite cartoon characters if you are auditioning for a comedy. If it is a drama, choose 2 super hero characters. You decide which one you will be and which one the casting director will be.

When you go into your audition, you will see Goofy and Bart Simpson or Spiderman and Black Widow or whomever you've chosen for the casting director and that's all you see. When you start your lines, pretend you are now reading with Goofy.

Exercise #3
Teach what you need to learn. By teaching others you will learn how to overcome your own fears.

Here are some ideas for you to consider:

- Work with kids in drama class.
- Work with kids who have a speech to do.
- Participate behind the scenes in your school performances.
- Volunteer your time at your local theater.
- Help your friends overcome their nerves.

Exercise #4

Read my blog, "Show Fear the Door" and read what Taylor Swift, Vanessa Hudgens and Justin Bieber said about combating fear.

http://thedrayway.com/blog/2012/01/show-fear-the-door/

You gain strength, courage, and confidence by every experience in which you really stop to look fear in the face. You must do the thing which you think you cannot do.
  - Eleanor Roosevelt,
  Former First Lady

The more opportunities you have to perform in front of people, the easier it becomes if you are ready.
  -Irene Dreayer

10
MEMORIZING IS NOT ACTING; ARE YOU BELIEVABLE?

Memorizing your lines does not mean you are a good actor; it's not enough. I have seen this over and over, again and again. Just because you say the words without looking at your pages does not mean you can act. I can recite the alphabet and the Pledge of Allegiance; that doesn't make me an actor! When you say your lines, you must understand exactly what you are saying. What does every word mean in your script? You have to know what the scene is about. You have to understand the characters, what they feel. And if you don't understand the scene, then you cannot connect with the material. Your performance is not honest; it's not sincere, and I can tell! So can everybody else.

If you don't understand what you are saying and you are simply reciting words, it shows. Your body language, your mannerisms and your inflections give away the fact that you have no idea what you are talking about or why! The biggest clue is that non-intentional sigh before a line! This tells me you are trying to remember your next line and how you should say it. Mom, when you are working with your child for an audition pay close attention when they say their lines. Does it sound memorized? Ask your child to summarize, in their own words, what's going on in the scene. Ask them to describe what their character is feeling and doing in the scene. I recommend you do this with an acting coach, but if not, make sure your child fully understands that each line requires a particular emotion.

I recently had a Skype session with an 11 yr. old singer from Canada who was auditioning for a music competition show for kids called "The It Factor." Her parents asked me, "What is the 'It' factor?" Before I answered their question, I wanted to hear the song the girl had chosen.

After singing a song by the Dixie Chicks called, "Wide Open Spaces", it was obvious to me that she did not understand the meaning of the song at all. She looked like a frozen popsicle that had memorized the lyrics. Aside from being shy and introverted, she was not showing any emotion or feeling when singing. I asked her, "Do you understand the story behind the song? Do you know what the words mean?" She admitted that SHE DID NOT!

I asked her what her second choice was and she told me it was a Justin Bieber song. She sang this song exactly the same way as the one before… frozen with no emotional connection. The first line of the song was, "Love it, feel it, believe it." I told her and her parents that the "It Factor" was right there in the first line of this song: Love, feel, believe… IT!

I told the girl to go to the bathroom and get her hairbrush. Then I had her turn off all the lights other than her computer. We discussed the words to her song, the meaning, the emotion and how it related to her life. I asked her to sing the songs again. With her hairbrush in hand, holding it like a microphone, and her computer as the spotlight, she sang as if she were performing at the Billboard Music Awards. OMG – she got it! She was able to tap into the emotion and the feeling because she understood the lyrics. The lights went on, and the parents were sitting there with their jaws dropped. They had never seen their daughter sing with such conviction. There's something in a hairbrush!

Are you believable when you are performing a monologue or a song? Does the audience believe what you are saying or are you just reciting? If you are performing a dance, do they feel your passion in your movement to the music? The audience needs to feel the same emotions that you are feeling. It is absolutely imperative that you understand the plot behind the story, the meaning of the lines, the significance of the lyrics to the song and the story behind the dance. If not, you have only memorized the words, the lyrics or the steps, and I will not believe you. Nor will your audience believe you. I always say, "If I *can't* tell you are acting, then that's acting."

You now understand that there is more than memorizing, and you must be believable when you act, sing or dance. You have to talk like a real person. Talk like you do with your mom, your BFF or your brother. Think about that when you are in a scene. When people speak naturally, their voices go up and down in a conversation and are not monotone (a continuing sound of someone's voice, that is unchanging in pitch and without intonation). If you sing Happy Birthday with only one note... go ahead try it! It's boring! Just like your conversation would be if it were all one note.

The most common fault that I witness, about 90% of the time, is when kids say their line and the last few words at the end of the sentence are barely audible. I can't hear you! When you drop the last few words in your sentences, you lose the impact of everything you have just said. Writers are paid a lot of money to write these words... ALL OF THEM! The most valuable information may be in the last two words of the line. It's a bad habit that I encounter all the time in casting sessions with kids. I refer to it as "going into the basement."

When I Skype with kids or meet them in person, I've heard many times that the character they were auditioning for was not like them. They couldn't relate to or identify with the character. They didn't think they did a good job. I skyped with a girl who had just finished such an audition. She told me that she didn't do very well. I asked her why not. She said, "The character was just not me. I would never behave or talk the way she did." I said to her, "That's called acting!"

After you say your line, don't stand there as if you were waiting for a bus. When the other person speaks, don't have a blank look on your face waiting for them to finish. You need to listen in character. You need to remain in the scene as the character you are portraying. If your lines are just memorized, you will not have that connection necessary to make the scene believable. Once, I was doing a scene with a boy and I could tell he was not paying attention to what was going on in the scene. Instead of continuing with my next line, I veered off course to determine if he was listening in character or even listening at all. I began to recite "Goldilocks and the Three Bears" instead of my next line. I said, "This bowl of porridge is too hot, and this bowl of porridge is too cold, and this bowl of porridge is just right." He responded with his memorized line without realizing I was talking about Goldilocks! He wasn't listening, not to mention not listening in character. All he cared about was to say his memorized line. That's not acting!

Many times in casting sessions, kids are asked to do the scene again, but with a change or addition of a word. I've seen it over and over that if a kid has only memorized his lines, this really throws him off. For example, the line reading is, "I've been waiting for you to show up all day." You are asked to repeat the line and this time add the words, "or mom." "I've been waiting for you or mom to show up all day." Unless you connect with the scene and understand what is going on, it's difficult for kids to re-adjust their memorized, rehearsed lines. When I Skype with kids, sometimes I stop them to re-do a line in the middle of a scene. When I ask them to continue, they are unable to unless they start from the beginning. Can you say or sing the alphabet and start with "J?"

By simply committing your lines to memory, without the understanding, you will get you nowhere.

Please watch these Drayism videos before proceeding to the exercises in this chapter:

Drayisms by The Dray - Memorizing Is Not Acting

http://youtu.be/mv2-O8vIo-s

Drayisms by The Dray - Sound Believable in Your Audition

http://youtu.be/3bD-j6e0JXY

Drayisms by The Dray - Memorizing Isn't Enough

http://youtu.be/civkTz1yYS8

Drayisms by The Dray - Now That's Acting

http://youtu.be/Uatz53fU9NM

Drayisms by the Dray - Don't End Sentences in the Basement

http://youtu.be/sKoXYnmVwUE

Exercise #1

This exercise is to help you avoid speaking like a robot and avoid using a monotone voice. When delivering your lines, you should sound the same way you do when you speak. When speaking, your voice normally goes up and down. You hit different notes when you speak, just like you do in a song.

Using the keys on a piano, chords on a guitar, a pitch-pipe or recorder, play a series of notes. Do not hit the same key on the piano or play the same chord on the guitar. Now, read your lines, matching the words to the different notes. Do this until you hear how your voice normally goes up and down.

Another way to do this exercise is to pick one of your favorite songs and recite your lines using the exact same notes as the song. If you love, "Rolling in the Deep" by Adele, recite your lines instead of the lyrics. You will notice that your voice naturally follows notes when you speak.

Exercise #2
I use the following exercise with all of my kids. Whether you are a novice or an experienced actor, this exercise will help you choose the emotion in a scene and understand what that emotion sounds like. It is also a great exercise to help you choose emotions in day-to-day situations.

First, write down 2 sentences about anything in your life, past, present or future.

For example:

a) My mom always picks me up after school. The other day she forgot, and I had to walk home.
b) My annoying little brother wants to be President of the United States. He tells everyone to vote for him and he's only 4 yrs. old.
c) Did you see that new sitcom on the Disney Channel? I hope one day to have my own TV show too.

Here are 20 emotions to choose from:

happy, sad, crying, shy, nervous, shocked, furious, confused, whiny, hysterically funny, surprised, disgusted, excited, suspicious, worried, love struck, paranoid, relieved, mischievous and puzzled.

Now, repeat the two lines you wrote (or from the examples above), incorporating a different emotion each time you say the lines.

Exercise #3
This exercise will be helpful when you are in a scene and your character is naming items in a list. The words need to sound like you are thinking of them right on the spot without sounding memorized.

If I asked you to name everything on the top shelf in your refrigerator in 10 seconds and without time to think, you would normally sound something like this:

Uh, orange juice..., um, milk, tuna fish..., uh water, mayonnaise...
Here are a few examples so you can practice. I'm sure you could come up with more if you need additional practice. In 10 seconds, can you:
Name everything in your top dresser drawer... GO!
Name your five favorite television shows... GO!
Name what you ate in the past two days... GO!
Name everything in your backpack (or purse)... GO!

Remember how you sounded when you listed the items above. You paused and had to think because the words were not memorized. Imagine the dialogue exchange below taken from your script. Apply the same pace and delivery when you answer my question:

The Dray (angry):
I've been waiting all day! Why are you late?
You (lying about your reasons): Well, my car didn't start, and there was traffic
and, then I had to go back to my office to get my briefcase aaaannnd the elevator got stuck, but... I'm here.

You don't have to memorize everything in this chapter, just:
Remember it, Learn it and Use it.
-Irene Dreayer

11
BIGGER AND LOUDER DO NOT MAKE YOU A BETTER ACTOR

Big, unnecessary, exaggerated and over-the-top moves and loud, screaming and deafening voices do not tell me or anybody that you are an incredible actor. The same applies to real life discussions and conversations; big gestures and loud voices are not always effective in getting your point across.

When you deliver a script line or in ordinary conversation, it is not necessary to over-exaggerate your body movements and make grand gestures. In an audition, ask yourself if you look like a symphony conductor, waving your arms, as you read your lines? In real life, are you conducting an orchestra when you converse with others? Are your unscripted gestures so over-the-top that you could knock over a vase on the set? This does not add to the quality of your acting to express a word or a line with huge arm movements and unnecessary overemphasized body actions.

For example, if your script says: "I have a huge problem!" You don't need to act out the word 'huge' by opening up your arms as far as they go – or even farther than that! Use your voice, not your arms, to act out the concept of 'huge.'

During one of my Dray Way sessions, a boy was reading a scene for me. One of the lines was, "My dad went fishing." While delivering that line, the boy pretended he had a fishing reel, and proceeded to imitate someone casting and reeling in a big fish... that's a big NO! The only time you would actually demonstrate "My dad went fishing" is if you were doing a "How To" video on "How to Catch a Fish." Oh, and by the way, if you reel one in... put it on rice because The Dray loves sushi!

There are two specific situations when you may be instructed to act out the meaning of a word or line. One instance would be a "stage direction" written in the script to advise the actors what they should be doing during the delivery of their lines. If the stage direction says "while jumping" then deliver the line while jumping up and down. The second situation would be if you were directed to do so. If your line is "Look at that bird," don't flap your arms like a bird, unless the director yells, "FLAP!"

During a rehearsal of an episode of "The Suite Life on Deck," the director gave instructions to all the extras (and by the way, an extra on a TV show or movie is just that, an extra person in the background of a scene, **not the star!**). He directed them to subtly "bop to the music" as if they were enjoying the groove and having a good time. One of the extras demonstrated what 'bop to the music' meant to her as she proceeded to act out what she thought was the direction. She imitated a person putting on headphones and then cranking up the volume. She then acted like the music was blaring in her ears and raised her arms above her head similar to an audience at a concert. Next, she continued to move her body to the music with full-out dance moves as if she were the opening act of "Cirque de Soleil!" Instead of simply moving her head or tapping her toe to the beat, she busted out in an exaggerated, over-the-top, unnecessary, ridiculous solo dance performance. I was given the job of going up to her and politely explaining what this "simple" direction meant... a little bop and a little toe tap. She was embarrassed but took the direction well.

Not all extras take direction well, as was the case with another extra on the set of "The Suite Life of Zack and Cody." A girl, hired as an extra, thought we would notice her more if she exaggerated her reactions to the dialogue of the main characters. She made unnecessary, over-the-top gestures with her arms to the simple line, "Oh, is he missing?" as if this were the worst disaster in mankind... simply to get our attention. By doing this, she hoped to get a better role or maybe even some dialogue! She was noticed alright, too noticed! We told her over and over that she needed to tone down her gestures. After many warnings from the director and after numerous takes (which is the number of times you do a scene), she was dismissed from the set for not taking the direction given to her.

During Skype sessions, I see kids trying to act the way the "bop to the music" girl did. Then I ask, "Who told you to do it that way?" Half the time they tell me "mom" and the other half they say "I was told in acting class." Acting coaches at these schools might teach you to over-exaggerate as a way for you to understand the story, the lines and the emotion. But, unless the stage direction or the director says otherwise, "bigger is not better" nor is it appropriate in an audition, a performance or in real life.

In the script, if there is a stage direction stating that you need to say the line in an *extremely loud voice*, then, that is exactly how you need to say the line. But if it is not written in the script or the director does not tell you to yell or scream, then don't... that's what the microphone is for... and we producers are not hard of hearing. Remember "less is more." Even if the character is angry, the volume doesn't necessarily have to be loud and over the top to get your point across. Your mom yelling at you to clean your room... now that's loud. Once again, less is more!

On numerous occasions, I have encountered this problem that kids have of yelling while delivering lines. I have seen it (or better said, HEARD IT) during Skype sessions and also during auditions for "The Suite Life of Zack and Cody." One boy began to say his lines at one of the auditions, and the unbelievable volume of his voice literally knocked me off my chair. I asked him, "Who told you to yell the lines?" He said, "My mom told me to use my outside voice." Tell your mom, "You are not at a football game!" Use your inside voice.

When you are working on stage in a play or Broadway musical, these rules "Bigger and Louder Do Not Make You a Better Actor" apply with two exceptions. First, if you are not provided a microphone, then you will need to project, not yell, as you deliver your lines. And secondly, gestures and facial expressions of the performers on stage in a large theatre tend to be grander than when the camera is directly in front of you. The reason for this is so the families in row "Q" of the balcony can see, hear and understand what is happening on stage.

If you have a tendency to over-exaggerate your gestures or to shout every word, these exercises should help you overcome your need to yell or act out the lines like you are playing charades.

Please watch this Drayism video before proceeding to the exercises in this chapter:

Drayisms by The Dray - Bigger Does Not Make a Better Actor

http://youtu.be/UwtHP_BMrSM

Exercise #1

Hold a 5 pound bag of sugar or flour in each hand. (Use a 5-pound weight if you are not a "Betty Crocker" or "Sara Lee.") This way, you are unable to gesticulate and must rely on your voice and facial expressions.

To deliver the following lines:

- "I saw this really huge bird flying over my head and then, guess what it did!" (No flapping!)
- "I'm going to audition for "So You Think You Can Dance" in one week." (Don't act out every dance you know and don't give me the finger... lol!)
- "When I opened the door, everyone jumped up and yelled, 'Surprise'!" (I bet you wanted to jump... but not necessary)
- "The boxer threw a left hook that knocked his opponent out." (No need to fall on the floor!)
- "The pitcher threw a super fast ball, and the batter hit that ball into the right field bleachers... Home Run!" (No throwing, no hitting and no running!)

Were you able to deliver the lines without gesturing? Are the pounds of sugar and the weights getting too heavy? OK, put them down, sit down, and sit on your hands. Again, use your voice and facial expressions to deliver these lines:

"Did you see that huge elephant? He must have been 8 feet tall and 20 feet long with a gigantic trunk and enormous floppy ears. He started running towards me, so I jumped out of his way and smacked him on the butt... hurt me more than it did him."

"I dreamt we were on this beautiful cruise ship, and suddenly the weather turned. *(And don't you dare turn your chair around!)* Huge clouds passed over the ship; lightning was all around us followed by loud claps of thunder. Then this wave came towards us... probably taller than the Empire State Building. I screamed, 'Oh no!' Well, that sure woke me up!"

OK, did you succeed? Now, let's move on to the "louder" exercise, but this time... no sugar, no weights! Phew!

Exercise # 2

Let's work on your habit of "blasting" your voice. You will find that you can get the emotion across just the same in a hushed manner. This exercise has proved to be successful with many of my Dray kids because it helps them to show the emotion without yelling. You will realize that "Louder is Not Better."

Pretend you are in a library with your scene partner. You can only deliver your lines in a strong whisper and without huge gestures. Or better yet, actually go to the library where you definitely can't be loud nor can you be disruptive and distracting with your sweeping gestures! Lower the volume of your dialogue with your partner and "Shhhh" your partner if they are too loud. Or the librarian will "Shush" you. Meanwhile, sit on your hands so you won't knock over a stack of books, and then you'll be in big trouble with the librarian. Remember, you must retain all of the emotion in the scene while maintaining the energy required as if you were speaking in a loud voice. You will find this amazing discovery: louder does not always relay the emotion.

PS: The library, do you know where it is?

I can take out my ear plugs now that you are not yelling. I can now move back to the front row knowing that you won't knock my glasses off with your exaggerated arm movements.

Bigger and louder do not make you a better actor but...
A subtle and accurate delivery of a line will make you a better actor.
Overcoming your tendency to use huge gestures will make you a better actor.
Knowing when to use the appropriate volume will make you a better actor.
Interpreting stage directions accurately will make you a better actor.

12
ACT DON'T POINT

Hasn't your mother ever told you that it is incorrect to point? Well, the same thing is true when you are acting. It is incorrect to point to the object that you are speaking about. Even in every-day conversations you may have with friends, family, teachers and even strangers, it is frowned upon to point.

Time and time again, I find myself correcting what "acting teachers" have taught kids. The teachers have told kids that, in order to get the point across, you have to point to the object to be more affective. As an Executive Producer, I witness this mistake in numerous casting sessions. It is not uncommon that inexperienced kid actors, or in fact any actor, may not have the confidence to allow their emotion and feeling to get the point across... without pointing.

So, when you audition or perform, every time you say the word "I," you don't have to point to your "eye" or to yourself... I know who "I" is! When speaking of your "heart," you don't have to show me where it is... I did well in anatomy. If the word "floor" is mentioned in a line, you don't need to point to it... I'm standing on it too. And if you are "hungry," you don't have to rub your tummy... I can hear your stomach growling! If you mention that you are "tired," it's not necessary to "yawn." After producing over 600 half-hours of television, I know what tired is!

During a Dray Way session, a girl was reading a scene for me. One of the lines was, "I love taking ballet class and wearing toe shoes." And guess what?

She pointed to her toe! Pointing to convey the meaning of every word in every line is totally not necessary, this is not charades!

Also, when you are in a scene, please refrain from pointing to objects that are mentioned in the other actor's dialogue. For example, if your scene partner's line is that he has a headache, you don't have to immediately point to your own head or will get a headache!

Speaking of headaches, I got one while watching a contestant auditioning on "American Idol." While singing, this guy "pointed" and gestured every other word of his song. I wanted to tell him: "Sing! Don't Point!" The emotion and tone of your voice, not your gestures, should convey the passion and feeling of your words. In this blog, http://thedrayway.com/blog/page/4/, you can compare the "American Idol" contestant with Adele singing "Someone Like You" in a live performance on "The David Letterman Show":

Adele - Someone Like You (Live on Letterman)

(http://youtu.be/ks_TWcupE6w)

You will see what I'm talking about. Adele conveys the emotion of the song in her voice without pointing!

There are times when a singer or actor may point to emphasize a word or sentiment. A situation where it would be appropriate is when the script specifically states that your character, for example, aggressively walks up to the other actor in a scene, *points to him* and says, "don't understand what am saying." Another situation to point would be to accentuate something of extreme importance. For example, the lyrics of a song are "My heart aches when I'm without you." The emotion would only be complete if you did place your hand on your heart. But remember, not every single word needs an action... it's distracting!

The first two exercises below can be done by yourself. But, if I may make a suggestion, they might be fun to do with a friend, your mom, dad, brother or sister.

And remember: NO POINTING, JUST ACTING!

Please watch this Drayism video before proceeding to the exercises in this chapter:

Drayisms by The Dray - Act, Don't Point

http://youtu.be/v5-uk4chov0

Exercise #1
Try communicating the following lines by using only the tone of your voice and facial expressions. But, first, sit it on your hands... both of them, so you can't use them to point when acting out these lines.

- I absolutely love to eat sushi. (And no pointing to your eye, heart or stomach.)
- Yuck! Sushi tastes like you are licking the bottom of an aquarium. (No sticking out your tongue and pointing to the bottom of the bowl)
- I'm nervous and scared about going on an airplane. (No nail-biting)
- I saw the teacher put on her glasses and open the book. (Don't point to any glasses or books)
- I wiped the sweat from my brow just before the panic set it. (Don't wipe... unless you really are sweating!)
- She smiled at me, batted her eyes and blew me a kiss. (She did it... don't you!)
- Do you think I need to get a haircut? (No hair pointing)
- I have a headache, my stomach hurts and I feel like I'm going to be sick. (Let your voice do the work here.)
- You have beautiful eyes and I love you with all my heart. ("Eye" - love - heart... Hope you got it by now!)

Exercise #2
Stand in front of the mirror or better yet, use a hand-held mirror. Practice showing these emotions without "playing charades." In other words, just use your facial expressions:

hungry, thirsty, scared, confused, surprised, excited, nervous, proud, disbelief, sad, happy, angry, disgusted, confident, ashamed, goofy, guilty, extremely sick, exhausted and... so tired... of making faces in the mirror!

Exercise #3
Try doing scenes on the phone with a friend. Since you can't see each other's face or hand gestures, you must rely on your voice to get the emotion across. Don't stop with just doing one scene. Practice several scenes: some dramatic, some comedic, and with a variety of emotions.

For additional practice, you will find a wide variety of scenes at these websites:

www.kidsinco.com/complete-list-of-playscripts or www.mocksides.com

This exercise also applies to the business world or the workplace. Let's say you are on a conference call with the big boss explaining a problem between YOU and HIM. Remember he can't see to whom you are pointing. Or, you are a salesman trying to convince a client that HE needs what YOU have. If you are heard and not seen, can you rely on your voice to "clinch the sale" simply by speaking?

Yes, there will be words that move you to point. That's fine, if, and only if the emotion is valid. But, as a precaution, that doesn't mean every single word. OK, you can get off your hands now... and wave good-bye!

Let your voice be your actions.
-Irene Dreayer

13
YA GOTTA, SPEAK CLEARLY

<u>Um, Ya Gotta, Speak, Like Clearly, Ya Know, at Your, Uh, Audition</u>

Ya know, I um coulda like written this whole chapter ya know like some people ya know um speak but I'm ya know not gonna! And um, do you like talk ya know this way? OK, that was difficult to write, since every other word was underlined in red, thank you spell check. I had to really think how to write those words. And that is exactly what you need to do when you speak; think about what you are going to say; have a plan in your mind; and stay one word ahead of yourself. But, that is easier said than done for most people. Too bad there's not a spell check for speaking.

I have met people that speak without saying "ya know" or "um" and would never use "gonna" or "havta." They have a command of their words, which shows confidence and assurance in who they are and in what they are saying. But, most of us use these pause words and these blended words. The pause words that we use that stop the flow of your sentence are called disfluencies. The blending of the sounds of words is called assimilations.

Sometimes the use of disfluencies and assimilations are okay. When you are talking to your friends, family and people you are familiar with it is accepted and overlooked. It's fine to use them when it is intentional; when it is purposely written in a song, advertising or a script. Bruno Mars uses "ya" in his famous award-winning song "Grenade" – not a problem.

Bruno Mars - Grenade [OFFICIAL VIDEO]

http://youtu.be/SR6iYWJxHqs. In fact, his song would just not sound right to say 'catch a grenade for you' as well as Brian McKnight's song "Shoulda Coulda Woulda." http://music.aol.com/video/shoulda-woulda-coulda/brian-mcknight/bc:11713031001 It is also accepted in advertising, as in the slogan 'I Coulda Had a V-8!' or Lay's potato chips 'Betcha Can't Eat Just One!'

In a script, if the writers use "I'm going to" or "You know I love you," then don't re-write the lines and say "I'm gonna" or "Ya know I love ya." If the script says, "Ya know I love ya" then that's exactly how you should say it, as it is in character.

It is not appropriate to use disfluencies and assimilations when delivering a speech or talking to your boss, a casting director, a producer, an interviewer; and when in a Skype session with me If you are doing a monologue or saying your lines, pausing and blending words shows me, as well as others, that you are not focused; you are nervous; and you are unsure of your lines. I witness this happening repeatedly with kids during my Skype sessions as well as casting sessions. I can understand the nerves because this might be the first time that they have ever spoken to a producer, casting director or anyone who might cast them. But, you absolutely need to be prepared, be focused and know the lines of your monologue or scene to avoid the and the *likes*.

I remember a casting session during "The Suite Life of Zack and Cody" when we were casting a young girl to play a love interest to Cody (Cole Sprouse). There was a line of girls waiting to read for this role. Cole came up to my office to say hi, but was more interested in looking at all the cute girls that were auditioning to play his love interest... at 14. On a whim, he walked into our casting session as we were about to bring in the next actress. She came in, and I really thought she was going to faint. She could barely speak since Cole was sitting right there. All of a sudden, all I heard was, "Like, um, ya know, like, uh, ya know!" When you lose your focus, and someone like Cole makes you nervous, you also lose your ability to speak correctly and adhere to what is written in the script.

During a Skype session, a young boy was saying his monologue. At the beginning and end of every sentence, he said either 'um' or 'uh' or 'well'. I could tell right away that he did not practice enough and was unsure of each and every sentence. Dude, learn your lines!

Aside from being nervous or lacking practice time, some people begin to use disfluencies and assimilations when they get excited. I was working with a girl to prepare for an audition. Before we began to practice her lines, she just had to tell me about a new guy she had a crush on. I realized that the only word I kept hearing was "like" and was missing the details of her story. She must have said the word "like" at least 20 times. After she finished the "like" story, I had to tell her. What's with all the "likes?" Do you like him? Does he like you? She told me that she has this bad habit. We continued working on her lines and then she began telling me about another audition she had. As soon as she said the word "like" (Oy! More "likes"), she backed up and started over. She, like, finally got it. Then, she stopped before she used the word "like." So, kids, listen to yourself and be aware of what you are saying.

We have all heard the familiar 'words' such as limo, fab, bro, perf. These terms have been incorporated and accepted into our culture and labeled as slang. Don't try to convince me that *"ya know, bro, um the limo ride was fab, like it was so ya know perf"* is correct. These slang words are considered acceptable in an informal situation and if written in your script. How would you properly describe your limo ride to your boss? "I would like you to know, sir, that the limousine ride was fabulous, so perfect!"

Another bad habit I hear constantly from kids (as well as adults) is 'Ya know!' Some people use the expression occasionally, yet many say it regularly as if it were part of every sentence. After the 50th "ya know," my response to them is: NO, I don't know! You don't realize you're saying this all the time, and it needs to be brought to your attention.

Most of us don't appreciate when others correct our speech or our grammar, so the best person to correct you is YOU!

Please watch this Drayism video before proceeding to the exercises in this chapter:

Drayisms by the Dray - Use Your Words Correctly

http://youtu.be/Va8AwT3cAK8

Exercise #1

This exercise will make YOU more aware of your own speech patterns as you listen to other people speaking.

Listen to your mom, your dad, a friend on the phone, a friend's conversation while sitting at McDonald's, your teachers at school or even interviews on TV. Keep track of the amount of times you hear anyone say a disfluency (ya know) or assimilation (gonna).

Now it's your turn. Have your parents or friends do the same for you.

Exercise #2
Create a scenario and begin to tell the story in SLOOOOOOW motion, and you are not allowed to use "um" "well" "like" or "ya know." Congratulations! You can do it.

Now, tell the story at normal speed and you should be able to catch yourself before your first "um."

Exercise #3
If just thinking about being aware of your speech is not enough, put a rubber band around your wrist. Every time you say "um" "ya know" "gotta" "like," snap the band! Ouch! Well, not too hard.

Exercise #4
Record yourself talking to your BFF on the phone (Just YOU... not your friend... that's illegal), telling a story about what happened at school, talking about your homework, rehearsing your monologue or describing how your little brother is driving you crazy. Count the number of disfluencies and assimilations you say. How did you do? Give yourself a grade. If you aren't happy with the grade you got, do it again.

Exercise #5
Number your paper from one to twenty. Write out the actual words that these slang words represent. Just remember which form of the words to use in which situation. The answers are below – no peeking!

1. abs
2. admin
3. ammo
4. app
5. info
6. intro
7. lab
8. legit
9. limo
10. max

11. memo
12. quads
13. sax
14. ump
15. veggy
16. vet
17. vibes
18. vocab
19. whiz
20. dray

Exercise #6
Read my blog "Speak Correctly in Your Audition":
http://thedrayway.com/blog/2012/03/speak-correctly-in-your-audition/

> Don't let your tongue outrace your brain.
> -Irene Dreayer
>
> The words you choose to say something are just as important
> as the decision to speak.
> -Anonymous
>
> It would be helpful if our mouths had a backspace key.
> -Irene Dreayer

Answers to Exercise #5

1. abdominals	2. Administration	3. Ammunition	4. Application
5. information	6. Introduction	7. Laboratory	8. Legitimate
9. limousine	10. Maximum	11. Memorandum	12. Quadriceps
13. saxophone	14. Umpire	15. Vegetable	16. Veterinarian
17. vibrations	18. Vocabulary	19. Wizard	20. Dreayer

14
CAN YOU FIND THE JOKE?

When you go in for an audition for a role on a situation comedy (sitcom), the most important word to remember is COMEDY. That means you are expected to be funny. How do you do that? First, you have to determine if your character is the funny one in the scene. Are you the one who delivers the joke? If so, can you find it? You won't see a big red arrow pointing to the line that screams, "Joke here!" It's there in black and white, and it's up to you to figure it out.

I've been in auditions with kids who say their lines but have no clue that what they just said was supposed to be funny. I've had to point out the joke and explain why it was funny. Finding the joke is really important because if you don't, the producers will hesitate to give you the job.

During one of my Skype sessions, I was working with a boy who had a huge audition for the lead in a pilot. After reading the scene with him for the first time, he had a problem finding the joke in the scene. His character was Wendell, an 11-year-old boy, the 'prince of dorkness.' His family recently moved to a new city and he was attending a new school. Here's the scene:

Wendell: (Approaching a group of kids at a table in the lunchroom) Look, I'm new here and just trying to make some friends. You can understand that, right? So maybe you can let me sit here for lunch. If it's not cool, just say the word.

(One kid dumps soup on Wendell's head)

Wendell: (Calm) Or do that. Well, luckily this isn't my first souping. I bring an extra set of clothes in my backpack. I only say that so you'll see I'm resourceful. A good quality in a frie-

(They pour more soup)

Bully: Let's go. Something stinks of dork.

Wendell: That could be the lentils. (End of scene)

I could tell he didn't find the joke! So, I asked him, "Do you know what lentils are?" He didn't know. That was the joke! Hello? Soup... stink... lentils... he missed it completely! Kids, if you don't know what a word means, ask your mother, your father, Daniel Webster or go to dictionary.com.

One way to find the joke when you read the scene is to pay attention to all of the lines in the scene, not just your own. Listen to the dialogue. It could be that another character's line is the set-up for your joke.

Here is an example of an actress paying attention to the other character's lines and using them to find her joke. One of the funniest scenes from an episode of "The Suite Life of Zack and Cody" was with London (Brenda Song) and Arwin (Brian Stepanek). As London entered the hotel lobby, Arwin was repairing the revolving door. London asked, "Whatcha doin'?" Arwin's answer was a long drawn out explanation (using every technical term related to every tool and their use) that went on and on. London listened intently to every single word that Arwin was saying and when he finished, London, after a long beat, repeated the same line, "Whatcha doin'?" We witnessed her ask the question, get an answer and process it as her character would. There was no punch line, but she found the joke and delivered it.

Another way to find the joke is to switch roles with the person reading with you, whether it is your acting coach, your mom, your friend or me, The Dray. When you switch roles, <u>you</u> now have the set-up line and your partner has the joke. As you say the lines of the other character, hopefully you will understand that their set-up line is a key to finding the joke. It's all about looking at the lines from another perspective. Now switch back to the character you are auditioning for and "ta-dah" you found the joke!

Many times the stage directions have clues as to where the joke is, as well as how you deliver the lines. So, carefully read all the stage directions in your script! A good example of this was taken from an episode of "The Amanda Show," a popular series from Nickelodeon, called: "The Boss's Office." (See exercise 3 for the sample episode)

Sometimes, in a scene, you don't have a line or a stage direction, but you still have to find the joke. It could be as simple as "a look." Carrie Martin, the mom on "Suite Life", could get the audience howling by looking at Dylan and Cole (Zack and Cody) and merely lifting one eyebrow. If your line is not the joke in the scene, it's all about your physical reaction. This can be just as funny, if not more. Brenda Song, Raven, Ashley Tisdale and Christian Wigg are all masters at being able to find the joke with just a look. "A look is worth a thousands words – or jokes!"

Can you find the joke in a difficult situation in everyday life? For example, your mom made a beautiful cake for her dinner party. She set the cake on the table in the kitchen. The house rule is that the family dog, a young Dalmatian, is not allowed in the kitchen. Oops, you forgot to close the kitchen door. Later, you heard your mom yell your name and from the sound of her voice, doom was pending. "Who let the dog in the kitchen?" your mom screamed. Yikes, it was you! It was an honest mistake and now you have to face your mom. No cake, filthy floor and a Dalmatian covered in butter cream icing. After you apologize, you say to yourself, there's got to be a joke here somewhere. "Mom, can't you see. He loved your cake. It hit the spots!" That made mom smile!

Finding the joke in a script can be like finding humor in life.

Please watch this Drayism video before proceeding to the exercises in this chapter:

Drayisms by The Dray - Can You Find the Joke in the Scene?

http://youtu.be/SKUJa1a0Huk

Here are some successfully proven exercises to practice finding and delivering the joke in the scene:

Exercise #1

This exercise will help you understand what 'funny' can sound like.

Get a newspaper and look for an article that is very serious, boring, of no interest to you or all of the above. Look in the business section, the front page, sports or the classified section. Read the story out loud to someone as if it were the funniest lines of a script you have ever read. It doesn't matter what the words are, concentrate on what funny sounds like. For example, how funny can you make this sentence sound: The gas company projects that, in the next fiscal year, gas will increase two-fold and create a severe hardship on our economy. Now, make that line funny!

Exercise #2

Now that you have an idea of what funny should sound and feel like, find a script that is actually funny. First, practice reading the entire script out loud including all of the other characters' parts. Then, read only one of the character's lines but not any of the others. Was that funny? Repeat reading the script and do the same with the other characters. Who has the funny lines? Who gives the set-up for the funny lines? And finally, ask yourself: Why is it funny?

You can find sample scenes at: www.mocksides.com

Exercise #3

This exercise will help you realize the importance of stage directions in understanding your role and what emotion is required.

A) Read the following lines out loud without the use of any stage directions in each of these lines:

Terry says:

Yes, you wanted to see me, sir?

Really? My goodness, I can't imagine what the problem could be.

What?! I swear, if I find out who said that, I will rip their lungs out through their stinkin' nose!!

Of course, you were saying?

Wh-what? I... I can't imagine who would say such a thing. Who said it?

Is this on tape? Do I look fat?

I don't have to take that kind of abuse!!

Oh, not at all, sir. Is there anything else?

What? I cannot believe that a person could be so hurtful as to say such mean and cruel and icky things about a human. It's so hurtful.

No. Yes. No. Yes. Sorta. Not really. Okay. Yes. No. Why do you ask? No. You wanna order pizza?

All right. You have discovered the truth. I am KGB spy, here to investigate you and your pasta primavera, Mister noodles and vegetables.

Don't you dare contradict me!!

B) Now, read Terry's lines in the script below out loud, paying attention to all the stage directions.

(Terry enters Mrs. Allen's office)

Mr. Allen

Terry. Come in

Terry

(Polite) Yes, you wanted to see me, sir?

Mr. Allen

Yes. Terry, there have been some complaints about you in the office.

Terry

Really? My goodness, I can't imagine what the problem could be.

Mr. Allen

Well, some people say you have a quick temper.

Terry

(Suddenly furious) What?! I swear, if I find out who said that, I will rip their lungs out through their stinkin' nose!!

Mr. Allen

Calm down

Terry

(Suddenly calm) Of course, you were saying?

Mr. Allen

Well, I also hear that you tend to be paranoid and insecure.

Terry

(Paranoid and insecure) Wh-what? (Chuckles nervously) I... I can't imagine who would say such a thing. Who said it? (Quickly looks around) Is this on tape? Do I look fat?

Mr. Allen

You look fine.

Terry

(Suddenly furious) I don't have to take that kind of abuse!!

Mr. Allen

So, no temper issues then?

Terry

(Totally calm) Oh, not at all, sir. Is there anything else?

Mr. Allen

Yes. It's also been brought to my attention that, sometimes, you can be a little... oversensitive.

Terry

(Crying) What? I cannot believe that a person could be so hurtful as to say such mean and cruel and icky things about a human. It's so hurtful.

Mr. Allen

Terry, is it true that you're seeing a psychiatrist for a split-personality disorder?

Terry

No. Yes. No. Yes. Sorta. Not really. Okay. yes. no. Why do you ask? No. You wanna order pizza?

Mr. Allen

Terry...

Terry

(Russian accent) All right. You have discovered the truth. I am KGB spy, here to investigate you and your pasta primavera, Mister noodles and vegetables.

Mr. Allen

You are <u>not</u> Russian.

Terry

(No accent, furious) Don't you dare contradict me!!

Were Terry's lines funnier once you followed these directions? How close were you to finding the funny?

Exercise #4

Find the Smiley Emoticons on your phone or computer (those yellow smiley faces). While standing in front of the mirror, mimic each one of these faces in a comedic way. Then, elicit the help of a friend or family member and see if they can: a) guess the emotion and b) do they laugh?

For more practice, go to www.google.com and search "emotion faces" in images. You will find pages and pages of a variety of real faces.

Exercise #5

What does funny look like? It's family game night! Invite your friends, your family and your neighbors – the more the merrier. Make two sets of cards. (Hint: Use 2 different colored index cards, one for the adjectives and one for the nouns.)

One set describes an emotion. The other set names a person or animal. Shuffle each set of cards separately. Divide the group of people into two teams. One team member picks a card from each stack, puts them together and acts it out. You cannot use your voice, only a facial expression and physical humor. Your team must guess what the cards say. Here is a list to get you started:

sad	clown
scary	monster
confused	senior citizen

uncoordinated	klutz
forgetful	dancer
terrified	singer
clumsy	juggler
nervous	pianist
worried	surgeon
happy	golfer
hungry	chef
tired	fish
angry	baby
dumb	dog

*When **life** gives you a hundred reasons to cry, show **life** that you have a thousand reasons to smile.*
-Anonymous

15
DON'T MAKE EXCUSES FOR A BAD PERFORMANCE

If you have a bad performance, don't blame the lights if they're too bright; don't blame the sound if you can't hear; don't blame the music if it's too loud; don't blame the time of day if this is when you nap; don't blame the audience if they're talking; don't blame the amount of time you had to practice because you had to study for a test; or don't blame your lack of sleep because the neighbor's dog barked all night. It just might be that you need to work harder to perfect your performance.

Mom, does your child make the same kind of excuses at home? Do they make excuses for not cleaning up their room, not doing their homework, coming home after curfew, not clearing their dishes from the table or for bringing home a poor test grade or report card? If the answer is yes; this can affect their auditions, as well as any goals they want to achieve in life. Kids, if you want to achieve any goal, you must have the desire that will push you toward your goal, but any excuses will pull you away. Take control of the situation and don't let the excuses control you. When you are truly committed to achieving something, you'll never give up, and you'll never give excuses.

J.R. Martinez, the army veteran, "All My Children" actor and the 2011 Season 13 "Dancing With the Stars" winner, does not make excuses. His life changed in 2003 while serving in Iraq when the truck he was driving hit a land mine and the subsequent explosion resulted in burns over 40 percent of his body. J.R.'s attitude is admirable, and after winning the mirror ball trophy he said, "My life didn't change in a tragic way, it changed in a beautiful way because I made a choice to change it… and go down that road that was open to me, and here I am today." He has been such an inspiration to kids all over the world who have faced similar adversities. He devotes himself to showing others the true value in making the most of every situation without making excuses.

Full story: http://www.accesshollywood.com/jr-martinez-wins-dancing-with-the-stars-season-13_article_57078

On the contrary, we have seen contestants on hit shows like "American Idol," "The Voice" and "X Factor" make excuses before and after their performances. It's as if they've given up before they've even started. You have to admire those contestants that, even though they didn't do as well as they could, didn't make excuses. They learned from the constructive criticism, accepted it and looked at it as an experience that will only add to their improvement. I admire them!

I've seen kids on You Tube start off their video with excuses and they hadn't even begun their song or monologue. Why would anybody want to watch? Remember, you can't give away what you don't give yourself. Practice saying this: This is going to be so good. I've practiced it, and you will love it. Tell yourself "I'm going to do a great job!" When you start off saying this is going to be bad, I've already moved on to the next video!

I had a client who used to make excuses during every audition she went on. She finally figured out that this was not a good thing when people in the room became restless and started looking for the exit signs. Once she realized that making excuses would get her nowhere, she created a plan. She decided if she really committed herself to learning her lines, she just might get the part and be successful. So, she wrote all her lines on index cards, put them in plastic baggies, and took them into the shower… soap and all, not to waste any time. She never gave another excuse for not knowing her lines. Rub a dub dub, learn your lines in the tub!

Kids, do these excuses sound familiar? They sound familiar to me because I personally have heard every one of them.

- I have a cold and a fever, so I might not sing this very well.
  My answer: THEN DON'T, do it when you're not sick!
- There is something wrong with the sound.
  My answer: WAIT until it gets fixed!
- I haven't learned the entire song yet.

My answer: STOP, learn the whole song first!
- I'm really tired so this monologue could be better.
  My answer: GO TO BED and record it after your nap!
- I wanted to play the guitar with the song, but a string broke.
  My answer: GO SHOPPING and record it later!
- The music is a little fast on this recording.
  My answer: SLOW IT DOWN or sing faster!
- This is not really my type of song (or monologue).
  My answer: PICK A DIFFERENT ONE, that suits you! DUH!

Please watch the Drayism video before proceeding to the exercises in this chapter:

Drayisms by The Dray - Don't Make Excuses for Bad Performances

http://youtu.be/vC-np-n-X2M

Now it's time for a few exercises. And don't give an excuse that you don't have time now because you have to go wash your hair or you need to post a joke on Facebook!

<u>Exercise #1</u>
For a period of a week, make a list of excuses that you hear other people say that begin with "I'm sorry" and another list of excuses that you use that begin with "I'm sorry." You will be more aware when you are about to make an excuse.

Here are some of the "I'm sorry" excuses you will probably hear:

I'm sorry. I didn't know it was my turn.
I'm sorry. I didn't know you were ready for me.
I'm sorry. Did you want me to go first?
I'm sorry. Could you repeat that?

<u>Exercise #2</u>
Make a list of all the excuses you have ever used in the past before, during and after an audition or performance. Then, throw the paper in the recycle bin as you throw your excuses away. But, please, don't recycle your excuses!

Here is a list of crazy excuses that I have heard in casting sessions on my shows from kids. Please, do not use them!

- I lost the script.
- I just got the new material.
- I'm hungry.
- I'm sick.
- I'm tired... would you believe I was up 'til 2am practicing?
- My dog ate the sides.
- I didn't have enough time to practice because I had to sell my Girl Scout cookies.
- I had to take my sister (brother, dog, etc.) to the doctor.
- I lost an hour on Daylight Savings Time.
- My mom locked the keys in the car, and my script was in there.
- I just had to watch a new episode of "Shake It Up" on TV.
- The music was too loud (too fast or too slow).
- My tap shoe broke.
- I didn't get a chance to break in my toe shoes.
- My fingers got stuck with Krazy Glue and I couldn't practice the piano (guitar).
- I had to put drops in my eyes and couldn't read the script.
- I had to put drops in my ears and couldn't hear the music.
- I returned a book to the library, and my script was in there.
- The spotlight was too bright.
- The spotlight was too dull.
- I couldn't find the spotlight.
- I thought the audition was tomorrow.
- I thought the audition was yesterday.
- I didn't know I had an audition.

No one ever excused his way to success!
-Anonymous

If you really want to do something, you'll find a way;
other people find excuses.
-Irene Dreayer

16
14 SHOULD LOOK 14

Headshots and Resumés

When you ask young kids how old they are, they show the number of years by their fingers, but they never fail to mention how many months, weeks or days until the next birthday. If you ask a kid who is six, his answer might be, "I'm six but I'll be seven in 3 months, 2 weeks and 4 days." He can't wait until his birthday. As kids become teens, they even want to tell people they are older than they really are. When you ask an adult, you won't see the finger count, but you might "get the finger!" If you get an answer, it might be the correct age, or most likely you will get a lower number, but never a higher number.

The rule in show business is that your 8 X 10 headshot needs to look like you! I'm serious; it must look exactly like you do now. It has to be current. You can't submit a headshot that was taken during your adorable and cute phase. That was 3 years ago, and you've changed. When casting sessions begin, all we have to go by are resumés and headshots submitted by your agent and manager. Based on the photo, you look perfect for the role that we are casting. If the role we are looking for is a 10-year-old with a specific look, we see your photo, and you look perfect for the part. So, we set an audition time for you to come in to audition, and we are looking forward to meeting you. Then you walk in the door, 13 with braces, a foot taller, and you look 20. Way too old for this role! Who is this person? You're not the person we saw in the picture. Where did that person go? Oh, you grew up! Now, you've wasted not just our time but your time as well. This is not fair to other kids. You might have taken another actor's opportunity to audition, who really looked the part.

When your headshots are so drastically different than how you look now, (it happens all the time) you are now obviously not right for the part. You must update them because you are constantly growing. Make them current so you continue to look like you, as your headshots are your calling cards for casting and auditions. Your headshot is not a driver's license picture that you are stuck with for four years!

Dray's Headshot Rules
Don't try to look older than you really are. You'll get there eventually.
Don't try to look younger than you really are. Been there. Done that.
Don't dress sexy. Toilet paper in the bra doesn't make you more talented.
Don't wear heavy make-up. It doesn't make you look older; it just makes you look like you are wearing heavy make-up.
Don't wear false eyelashes. It doesn't help you to stand out.
Don't wear sophisticated hairstyles. This is not "Tots and Tiaras."
Don't take a goofy picture. It limits you to only goofy roles.
http://sizis.com/media/images/29_1346_goofy-01.gif
Don't hold a baseball bat. Oh, are you an all-star little league player?
Don't hold a guitar. Are you appearing at "House of Blues?" Can I get tickets?
Don't airbrush your photo. Nobody is perfect! (Or no ""body" is perfect)
Don't substitute your "other twin" in the photo. The Dray, The "Twin Master" can tell.

Your school pictures, your yearbook pictures, your Bar Mitzvah or Bat Mitzvah pictures, your *Quinceañera* picture, your Facebook picture, your graduation picture, your passport photo, your company I.D. photo, your online dating photo and your headshot should look like you, not what you aspire to look like, but YOU!

Mom, before your kids take their headshots, it is up to you to make the decisions on what is appropriate regarding hair, makeup and wardrobe. Sometimes they want to look older, sexier and present an entirely different image than who they really are. Set boundaries on what is appropriate for their age, including how they are dressed for school. Mom, don't try to have your kid dress like you... they're not "mini-me's."

Mom, funny story: I was in a dressing room trying on a pair of jeans in Beverly Hills. I overheard a mom and daughter in the dressing room next to me having a discussion on what the mom thought was appropriate for school. The mom said, "You are NOT wearing that to school, or anywhere, you're too young." The daughter replied, "I'm 14, it's what everyone is wearing." Mom said, "It's not what my daughter is wearing." The daughter challenged her and said, "Well, you did, and you still do." Their conversation was quite loud, and I couldn't help from over-hearing them. I thought, I know that voice. We all walked out of the dressing rooms simultaneously, and there was mom, in all her provocative glory... the Divine Ms. Bette Midler! Even she knows what's age appropriate!

On the back of your headshot is your resumé. When you were in second grade and you got the role as the third munchkin in "The Wizard of Oz," in Springfield Elementary, please, don't put that on your resumé.

Dray's Resumé Rules
Don't lie on your résumé. We check. Trust me.
Don't list plays where you had no lines. We will want to know what role you played?
Don't list elementary school productions when you were seven. And your now 17 in high school? Who cares!
Don't list a credit on a TV show or pilot when you were an extra. Careful, I might have produced that show or pilot.
Don't list a credit on a movie when you were just the intern. And your role on the film was… getting coffee?
Don't list that you play piano when you only can play "Chopsticks." There's a piano in the next room; let's hear you play.
Don't list that you ride horses only because your Dad has one. The producer might invite you to his stable or write a horse into your role.
Don't list commercials "on request" if you've only done two. OK, I'm requesting.
Don't add your website address. No one will look.
Don't list your personal phone number. No agent? No manager? OK, then list your personal number.

The same rules apply whether you and your parents are meeting me or any other Executive Producer. This is called a "meet and greet", and I want to meet the real you. I had a meeting in my office with a 14-year-old girl. She was very pretty but there were two bats in the room… her set of eyelashes! False eyelashes – just like her mom. We talked about her goals, and I worked with her on a few scenes, but I was so distracted. I had to stop. I asked her, "Why are you wearing false eyelashes?" She told me, "I thought I would stand out more." She stood out, but for the wrong reasons. I said, "Take them off." She did, and the mother gasped. I explained to both of them, **14 SHOULD LOOK 14!** If she were going to stand out, it would be because she was a great actress.

Kids, if you think trying to look older will get you the job, it won't. If there is an 18-year-old girl who looks 14 and is a good actress, she will more than likely get the job over you. There are union restrictions on minors, due to required school hours and time limits, so looking older is not always going to help. The older actor who looks younger will get the job over the younger actor trying to look older. There are TV shows ("90210" and "Glee") and movies where the leads, playing high school students, are in their 20's. And that's just the way it is. If everybody is 20 playing 16, it works!

Kids, when you come in to audition for a role, it's OK to dress for the part but not mandatory. If the role is a country boy or girl that lives on a farm, there is nothing wrong with wearing overalls in your audition. Debby Ryan dressed the part when she auditioned for the role of Bailey on "The Suite Life on Deck." The role was a country girl from Kettlecorn, Kansas, and she looked like she just came in off the farm.

During a casting session for another role on "The Suite Life on Deck," a young guy came in to audition as one of the students in the "Semester at Sea" school. He was a bit overweight, braces, wild curly hair and bad skin. He gave the best audition and was exactly what we were looking for. We hired him exactly as is! We loved his weight, his braces and curly hair, and the rest we covered with makeup.

Don't hide what you think are imperfections. You just might be exactly what we are looking for, exactly how you are!

Please watch this Drayism before proceeding to the exercises in this chapter:

Drayisms by The Dray - 14 Should Look 14

http://youtu.be/WJF4Sql6K0E

Exercise #1
Girls, this exercise is for you. This is the Dray Way skin care regimen:

Take an up-close picture of your face before you put on makeup or do your hair.

Remember, we are talking about headshots. Here are my step-by-step suggestions for putting on make-up for your headshots. It's OK to highlight your positive attributes, but remember, keep them in check, "less is more."

- Start with a "clean canvas" by washing your face with a product that is designed for your skin type.
- Exfoliate: This means to wash with a granular cosmetic preparation in order to remove dead cells from the skin's surface. Please read this helpful article on how and why to exfoliate: www.mamashealth.com/skincare/exfoliate.asp
- Moisturize, moisturize, moisturize with a cream that works with your skin type.
- Use a soft blush color on your cheeks, not too much or you will look like a clown.
- Use a light-colored lip gloss.
- Whatever makeup you choose, it must be age appropriate. Remember, **14 SHOULD LOOK 14!**

Now, as you look in the mirror holding that picture up next to your face, ask yourself... Do I look like me? The same applies with choosing your hairstyle and your clothes. It's OK to look pretty, but don't hide your natural beauty behind heavy make-up, ridiculous hairstyles and overly-outrageous clothes.

<u>Exercise #2</u>

Boys, this exercise is for you. This is the Dray Way skin care regimen:

Take an up-close picture of your face before you put goo in your hair. Remember we are talking about headshots. Here are my step-by step-suggestions. It's OK to highlight your positive attributes, but remember, keep them in check, "less is more."

- Start with a "clean canvas" by washing your face with a product that is designed for your skin type. Boys, you have one face. You need to know how to take care of it. At your age, there are many skin problems you need to avoid.

- Exfoliate: This means to wash with a granular preparation in order to remove dead cells from the skin's surface. Please read this helpful article on how and why to exfoliate: www.mamashealth.com/skincare/exfoliate.asp
- Moisturize! Guys don't avoid this. Trust me.
- Skip the make-up unless you are filming on a set or you've become a member of the rock band, "Kiss."
- Remember, **14 SHOULD LOOK 14**

Now, as you look in the mirror holding that picture up next to your face, ask yourself... Do I look like me? The same applies with choosing your hairstyle and your clothes.

Who you think you want to be, might be less than who you are!
-Anonymous

17
I'D RATHER HAVE A SLOW 'YES' THAN A FAST 'NO'

Patience is defined as "the capacity to accept or tolerate delay, trouble, or suffering without getting angry or upset." - New Oxford American Dictionary

My dear parents, I have come to understand your struggle with being patient. We witness day to day, those people that hit the elevator button 42 times before it arrives. Those who wait at the corner to cross the street, hit the cross button 37 times, as well as those people with a slow computer who click on an icon 8 times. It doesn't make things happen faster and yet, sometimes, it makes us feel like we are forcing something to happen quickly. So, let's say your child had an audition at 2:00 pm on Monday. Do you begin to push that button over and over again to their agent or manager asking, "Do you know?" "Did you hear back?" "What did they say?" Like anything else, you must have patience. The elevator will eventually come, the traffic light will ultimately turn green, the website will appear, and you will get an answer about the audition when a decision has been made.

This same "patience" principal also applies whether your child tries out for a school play, the band, the soccer team or cheerleading; waits for the college acceptance letter; or if your child applies for a job. And parents, if you were interviewing for a job with Donald Trump, would you call him every day and ask, "Did I Get It?" "Did I get it?" His response would automatically be, "You're fired!" In this day and age, everyone expects answers immediately. People want answers to emails within minutes. Then there is "texting" where you want an answer instantly. We get annoyed when we have to wait on the phone and listen to computers ask us a million questions before we get to speak with a real person. Patience people patience!

An agent I worked with had a client who wanted to direct an episode of my Disney Channel Show "The Suite Life." The agent called me every day, no really, every single day and sometimes twice a day. "Did you hear yet?" "Do you have an answer?" "Can you give him an episode?" I told him, every time he called, that I was waiting for network approval before I could set up a meeting. He wasn't satisfied with that answer, and having no patience, he began to call all of my writers and my line producer asking the same questions. He even called other cast members trying to get information. We had a network meeting, and we collectively decided not to give the director the job. He wasn't qualified, and the agent who drove everybody nuts didn't help the situation! This is an example of a "slow no." But, there are many times, when you wait for that slow 'yes,' patience will pay off.

When your child goes for an audition, there are many people who must weigh in on the decision before there is a 'yes' or a 'no.' First, casting executives have to say yes. Then, producers have to say yes. Then, the writers have to say yes. Then the studio has to say yes. And finally, the network has to say yes. That's a lot people that have to talk about your child. Remember, there are many shows on that network; many kids who have auditions for roles on other shows. That's a lot of people waiting for a yes. So by calling your agent or your manager and constantly asking, "Did you hear? Did you hear? Did you hear?" doesn't help speed up the process. The only thing you will accomplish is annoying your agent or manager and eventually me.

Don't be a nag!

Sometimes "Yes" takes a really long time. A young boy auditioned for a role on "The Suite Life of Zack and Cody", and he was great. We had to postpone the episode to a later date due to one of the cast members shooting a movie. The impatience began with the barrage of phone calls looking for an answer. It might have been easier if I had just given him the fast 'no.' They couldn't understand that there might be a slow 'yes' due to the postponement. Guess what? He did get the job, but weeks later. This family got that slow 'yes', and I got a big pain in my you know what! I felt bad for the agent. The mom insisted he call me every day. "Did he get it?" "Did he get it?" Mom finally realized that she would rather have a slow 'yes' than a fast 'no.' As a result of that slow 'yes,' he subsequently became a regular on the series "Parenthood."

Parents, beware, you must be patient. Your anxiety about whether or not your kid got the job could prevent him from getting the job. We hired a young boy for one episode on "The Suite Life" with the potential of being a recurring character. He did a good job, but the impatience of the mother calling and calling and asking and asking, "Will he be back?" "Will he be back?" killed the deal. My heart went out to the child, but his mother and the constant nagging was not something the studio was willing to tolerate.

Your child may come out of an audition saying, "They said I was great." This does not mean that they got the job. This does not mean you should call your agent twice a day for a week! The casting directors and producers are nice people and always give encouragement at the end of an audition. "You did great" or "good job" does not mean "go to the bank."

Selena Gomez got the lead for a pilot I produced called, "Housebroken," one of the best pilots I've ever produced. We were casting for the role of her "best friend" and there were two actresses being considered for the role. The girl that did not get the job was awarded the lead of another pilot, which ended up being a hit series on ABC Family. Congratulations Cassie Scerbo! She waited for the slow "yes." It really paid off!

Please watch this Drayism video before proceeding to the exercise in this chapter:

Drayisms by the Dray - A Slow "Yes" is Better Than a Fast "No"

http://youtu.be/y6mHG1nhQ54

Exercise
Kids and parents:

Every time you, your mom or dad get the urge to call your agent day and night and day, do one, two or all of the following:

- Take a walk
- Take the dog for a walk
- Wash the dog
- Wash the car
- Call your grandmother
- Call your boyfriend or girlfriend
- Go to a movie
- Go to the park

- Go to the beach
- Change the oil in the car
- Practice the piano, guitar, dance routine
- Bake a cake
- Roast a turkey
- Read a book
- Read a magazine
- Mow the lawn
- Do your homework
- Clean your room
- Clean my room
- Have a designated friend willing to listen to you and call them instead of the agent
- And most importantly, rehearse for your next audition!

The longer you have to wait for something,
the more you will appreciate it when it finally arrives.
-Anonymous

18
IT'S EASY TO GET IN THE DOOR, HARDER TO GET BACK IN

So many times parents are extremely anxious to get their kid an agent and go to auditions when the child is not really ready. With the right connections, sometimes doors can easily be opened for you. Let's say you get an audition or a meeting because your agent said you were, by far, the funniest, the most talented comedic actor. When you arrive at the moment of truth, you begin your audition and, whoops! Your talent does not match the hype that was given by your agent... not even close. Even if you've improved over time, sometimes it's harder to get another chance to prove that you actually have gotten better! First impressions count!

Parents, this same rule, "It's easy to get in the door, harder to get back in" applies to every chapter in your child's life. Before your child attempts any activity, they need to be prepared from the start. Would you have your child try out for the football team even though they don't know how to throw a football? Would you have your child audition for the school band after only a few lessons on the tuba? Then you shouldn't push them into an audition or a sport or the band without being ready; they must have the skills. First impressions are once again very important; there might not be a second chance.

You audition your entire life. You audition for the cheerleading team. You audition to be class President. You audition for a sorority or fraternity. You audition for a job. You even audition on a blind date. If you lack the confidence and skills, it may be very hard to get back in for a second chance or maybe the door will be closed for good. Whether you audition for the school play or you audition to get a promotion in your company, you must be groomed and ready the very first opportunity you get.

An agent was selling me really hard on a particular client of his. He was raving about how his new client was such a fantastic and extremely funny actor. I took the agent's opinion as the truth and had no reason not to. I got the actor "in the door" to audition for a role in front of the writers, the directors and the network. As he was about to begin his scene, I noticed him sweating, fidgeting and physically shaking and then froze like "a deer in headlights" and that was not part of the audition. "Oy" I said to myself, this is not the incredible actor I was sold on. I wanted my money back or at least a credit! I practically dove under my chair and couldn't wait to call his agent and say, "REALLY?" Months later, his agent contacted me again to tell me how much better he had become and that he was now really ready. Because I'm a nice person, I was willing to give him another chance. I observed the actor doing a scene and guess what? He was ready and he was very good! I approached my producers and the network and explained how much this actor had improved. At first, they didn't even want to see him. But, I didn't give up on him, and as hard as it was, I got him a second chance. Not everyone will fight for you, even if you have become quite good.

Once you get "in the door", don't jeopardize your job and future opportunities, as did a young teenage client I once managed. He got a job as one of the regular characters on a new Fox series. During an episode, the director was ready to begin shooting a scene and my client was missing. I had warned him previously about constantly being late to the set and that he could lose his job. I called everywhere (hair and make-up room, wardrobe, craft services, his dressing room) but he could not be found and did not answer his cell phone. Where was he? He was nowhere on the set or in the vicinity. We had to send a P.A. (Producer's Assistant) to his home. They finally found him asleep in his bed and under the influence of drugs! He was fired from the show, and it has been extremely, if not impossibly hard for him to get back "in any door."

Whether you are famous or not, it's very difficult to get back in the business once you have faltered. Brittney Spears is a classic example of a star that made wrong choices, took a very wrong turn and paid the consequences when her career took a nosedive. She is now on her way to a second chance at a successful career. She got back in the door, but not without hard work, devotion and perseverance. But that door is not always wide open. Lindsay Lohan is having an extremely difficult time getting back in the door. Few companies want to take the high risk of hiring her for many reasons: insurance issues, constantly late, honesty in question, preparedness and will this happen again? But, Lindsay, we're rooting for you.

Please watch this Drayism video before proceeding to the exercise in this chapter:

Drayisms by The Dray - It's Easy to Get In, Harder to Get Back In

http://youtu.be/-HdUtuTg-xM

As your teacher and mentor, I am giving you and your child the night off from completing any exercises. No homework! Yeah!

> *There is no short cut to achievement. Life requires thorough preparation – veneer isn't worth anything.*
> —George Washington Carver

19
SUCCESS IS NOT PERMANENT

Never stop working after success and never stop trying after failure.

After a great audition, you get a role on a TV series. Success! Congrats! Oops, the show was moved to another night and a different time slot. The ratings dropped and the show was cancelled. Success is not permanent! There are other successes in life that are n<u>ot</u> permanent such as having a boyfriend or girlfriend. What happens when their family ends up moving across the country? Your relationship becomes "GU" – geographically undesirable. Or, let's say you've made first string on the football team, but end up on the bench due to a broken foot. Another success that is not permanent would be if you were hired to be the manager of a new restaurant and you lose your job because the restaurant closes.

I've witnessed many families that have given up everything and made the big move to Hollywood as soon as their child gets a role on a new TV series. WAIT! Hold on a minute. Not to be negative, but there's no guarantee that this show will be successful. What you should have done was waited for the first season to end. Or better yet, waited until the second season to see if the show continues. Parents, be patient and get more episodes under your belt. Remember a bad time slot could mean low ratings and a cancellation or your child's role could get written out of the show. What if unhappy actors walk off the show demanding more money or the star becomes ill and can't continue on the series? Another reason is money! A TV show, a feature film or a

Broadway show all need to make money to survive and no support from advertisers, no butts in seats and poor reviews lead to CANCELLATION!

There are big television network shows with star talent, huge budgets, top writers and tremendous promotion. But, every season new shows get cancelled. Some are cancelled as early as the third or fourth episode. Not so permanent!

Here are a few examples from the 2011 season:

How to Be a Gentleman(CBS)
Ending after three episodes, final episode on 10/15/2011
Free Agents(NBC)
Ending after four episodes, final episode on 10/5/2011
Charlie's Angels(ABC)
Ending after eight episodes, final episode on 11/10/2011
Terra Nova(FOX)
Ending after one season, final episode on 12/19/2011
The Defenders(CBS)
Ending after one season, final episode on 3/11/2011
Hellcats(CW)
Ending after one season, final episode on 5/17/2011
Better with You(ABC)
Ending after one season, final episode on 5/11/2011

If you are lucky, your series could go on for years. But, as they say, all good things do come to an end. The following shows went on for a number of years:

Desperate Housewives(ABC)
Ending after eight seasons, final episode on 5/20/2012
Smallville(CW)
Ending after ten seasons, final episode on 5/13/2011
All My Children (ABC)
Ending after forty-one seasons, final episode on 9/23/2011

Two shows that I produced had very successful runs and became syndicated (shows that reach 100 episodes are sold across the country to independent networks). "Sister Sister" ran for 6 seasons from 1994–1999 and after 120 episodes, the show is still popular throughout the world. "The Suite Life" Disney franchise aired for 6 seasons from 2005 to 2011 and every one of the 162 episodes remains popular in the U.S. as well as over 30 countries around the world.

On the other hand, there are successes in life that <u>are</u> permanent such as learning how to ride a bike (something you never forget), learning how to tie your shoe (You did it then; you can do it now.) and graduating from school (They can't take that diploma away from you.). But show business is not like tying your shoe. TV series, movies and Broadway shows all have a guarantee that they will eventually come to an end.

What is your next step when you find out your show is being cancelled or ending? After the tears and disappointment, you should already have a back-up plan in place. Anytime you are working on a show, you have to have the state of mind that this is going to end. Part of your plan is to continue taking classes even though you are employed. Successful doctors, teachers, chefs and other professionals continue to take classes to always improve and update their skills. Athletes are constantly practicing and working out to remain at the height of their game. As an actor, singer or dancer, you need to do the same in order to be ready for the next job.

Parents, you need to live within your means. When your child gets a job, it doesn't mean you should buy that big mansion, an expensive car or tons of clothes. A surprise cancellation could leave your family with nothing except a big mortgage to pay. Parents, legally your child's money must be deposited into a Coogan account (see exercise #3) where access is given only to your child when they turn 18 years old. In the meantime, don't spend money you don't have. And kids, when you do turn 18, my advice to you is SAVE YOUR MONEY. Bills are permanent, success is not!

Your back-up plan should also include diversifying your skills into other areas. If you are a singer, try writing. If you are a kid actor, try directing a play at camp. If you play an instrument, learn how to play another one. If you are a dancer, take an acting class. Constantly reach out beyond your comfort zone. Have the courage to learn.

Fred Savage, from the popular show "The Wonder Years" and the feature film "Princess Bride," began his back-up plan by directing Disney Channel shows like "Hannah Montana," "That's So Raven" and "Wizards of Waverly Place." He also produced "Phil of the Future" on the Disney Channel.

Phil Lewis, Mr. Moseby on "The Suite Life of Zack and Cody" and "The Suite Life on Deck," knew his role on these shows would some day end. As his back-up plan, he too chose to expand his résumé by learning the skills to become a director. He went on to direct several episodes of the "Suite Life"

Franchise. When the series ended, he was hired to direct many episodes of other Disney Channel shows, such as "Jessie," "Good Luck Charlie," A.N.T. Farm," and "Austin & Ally." Way to go Phil!

Mom, communicate with your child's representative and suggest that your child be considered for other types of projects. Some of these they might not have done before, such as commercials, voice-overs for animation, personal appearances and industrials. Your child needs to have the experience in other areas so they have a back-up to their current job.

Brian Stepanek, Arwin on "The Suite Life," became very successful in the commercial world while making us laugh as the bumbling, nerdy maintenance "engineer." When "Suite Life" ended, he too had a back-up career before, during and after his Disney success.

The biggest and most important part of your back-up plan is EDUCATION! Let me say that again. Your child needs an education! Show business is not always a permanent career. High school diploma – a must! College diploma – a must! And parents, schooling is imperative for all kids 6–18 yrs. old on a series or in a movie. Class attendance for a minimum of 3 hours is mandatory on set or on location. If your child has graduated from high school and is working on a show, they can still pursue a college education, albeit online or attending classes at a local college.

Tia and Tamera Mowry, from my show "Sister Sister" ("Twitches", "Tia & Tamera") started college during the last few years of the show. As stated in a 1998 article from Ebony Magazine, "Juggling acting with academics is all in a day's work for the 20-year-old identical twins. As third-year students, Tia and Tamera take part-time classes together, then drive to the set of their WB sitcom to tape episodes." I was so proud that they continued their studies after the show ended and graduated from Pepperdine University with high honors and degrees in psychology.

Who are the first Disney Channel stars to go to college? If you said Dylan and Cole Sprouse, of my shows "The Suite Life of Zack and Cody" and "The Suite Life on Deck," then you are absolutely right. After working with them for 6 years, I felt like my own kids were leaving the nest when they left for college. Dylan and Cole knew that acting was not always a permanent career, and they wanted a back-up plan to get a college degree as well as wanting to expand their horizon.

Failure and success is the product of the same process. There are those that are permanent and those that are not. You failed a test, but you haven't failed the class. Your restaurant opened and failed to get good reviews, but you now know what to change to make it a success. You failed to win the marathon, but you successfully crossed that finish line. You failed to get the lead in a movie, but you succeeded in getting another role. Your show is over, but your career is not. Just like success, failure is not permanent.

Mom and Dad, if your child's show is cancelled, you need to help your child deal with the disappointment with dignity, understanding and sensitivity. It will help them move on to the next project – which might be even bigger. Failure can be turned into new dreams, new hopes and eventually new successes. The only way failure can be permanent is if you and your child choose to quit.

When your TV show is cancelled, you have been written out of a feature film or the Broadway show you were in closed, think of it as a temporary setback and also a learning experience. If you didn't have a back-up plan, learn from this and start your plan now and make your setback a comeback.

Your dream of becoming a successful star has come true, and your name is in lights. But, don't forget that any success you might have, in show business and in life, may not go on forever. Always be looking for and working on the next challenge, the next audition and the next chapter in your life.

Never stop working after success and never stop trying after failure. Remember that, learn that and use that!

Please watch this Drayism video before proceeding to the exercises in this chapter:

Drayisms by The Dray - Success Is Not Permanent

http://youtu.be/gH5f3Y6_mMk

Exercise #1

If you were not an actor, singer, dancer or musician, or aspiring to be one, what would you do instead? Whether you have a plan to enter show business or not, this exercise will help you see what options you have.
1. Write down 3 college classes you would take that interest you.
2. Write down 3 jobs or careers you are interested in.
3. If you could open your own business, list 3 types of businesses you would open.
4. Choose 3 other areas of show business that might interest you: director, producer, writer, make-up artist, wardrobe, lights, camera, stage manager, talent agent, talent manager, publicist, editor or casting.

5. List 3 hobbies or sports that you currently have.
6. List 3 hobbies or sports that you might be interested in starting.
7. List any other interests that you have.
8. Now, highlight any elements of the above lists that require additional training or education? With the help of your parents, investigate how to get that training or education, where you would go and how much it would cost it.

Good luck in whatever career path you choose, but always have that back-up plan.

Exercise #2
Read my blog about Dylan and Cole Sprouse attending college plus other celebrities like Tia and Tamera Mowry who earned college degrees: http://thedrayway.com/blog/2011/07/the-suite-life-zack-cody-go-off-to-college/

Exercise #3
Success is knowledge. It's important that you understand all aspects of the business. Watch the Dray Way webinar "The Business of the Business – Part 2" regarding the Coogan account and your child's earnings: http://thedrayway.com/webinar-business2.html

Read about the California Child Actor's Bill, also known as Coogan Act or Coogan Bill: http://www.sag.org/content/coogan-law

Success is not the end, but the beginning of your next successes.
-Anonymous

20
FINAL THOUGHTS FROM THE DRAY

Congratulations! If you are reading this then you have completed the book, done the work, and now you are ready to make decisions and use The Dray Way on your path to success.

You've renamed rejection, found the joke, learned to act not point, shown fear the door, kept focused and defined whose dream this is. And parents, you are now armed with the skills and knowledge to be a terrific CEO!

Mom, Dad, I have one more very important exercise for you and your child to complete. But, before answering the following questions, make sure you have read all the chapters, completed all the exercises and watched all the Drayism videos.

Your Final Exercise!
Ask yourself these questions and be honest with yourself. If your answers are all "YES" then you are ready to get in the door and pursue that dream. If any of your answers are "NO," go back and reread this book and repeat the exercises until you can answer all these questions, "ABSOLUTELY YES!!"

Kids, these questions are for you to answer
Will I remember you?
Do you look your age?
Do you take your career seriously?

Do you train and practice all the time?
Do you speak clearly?
Do you really understand what you are saying in a scene (or song)?
If it is a funny scene, can you find the joke?
Are you focused in an audition?
Are you confident and able to leave nerves and fear 'at the door?'
When you act (or sing), will I believe you?
Are you able to show the emotions with just your face?
Can you portray emotions in your voice?
Are you willing to be patient?
Are you willing to put in that extra "umph"?
Aside from your education, will your show business career be your #1 priority?
Is this your dream and not your parents'?

Mom, Dad
Will you support your child in pursuing their dream?
Will you provide the means for them to take classes?
Will you assist your child in performing everywhere they can?
Will you allow them to audition, but only when they are ready?
Will you keep your child focused in an audition?
Will you remain in the background in the audition room and on the set?
Can you accept your child's rejection and provide support for them?
Have you done your homework as the CEO?

All yeses? You are now ready to go to that audition and be FABULOUS!
See you on set!
The Dray

GLOSSARY

Definitions of Industry Terms & Lingo

assimilations - Words formed from the blending of sounds, like wanna (want to), shoulda (should have) or gotta (got to).

callback - When your child has read for casting agents and they want to bring you back in to read for the producers, that is a callback. They "CALL YOU BACK" to read again. This is one step closer to being approved by the network and booking the job. It is a big 'yay' if you get a callback.

call time - The time you are to report for hair and make-up or on the set. Plan to be early so you have time to park, find the studio (if it is your first time) and get your child settled. If your call time is 10:00am, don't come flying in the door at 9:58am!

camera blocking - The director instructs all of his camera operators where and when to shoot. Blocking is usually done prior to the actual shooting of a scene.

Sometimes the actors are in the scene, or they have stand-ins that "stand in" for the actors as the director and camera operators go through this process.

casting director - They are hired by the producers of a TV series and network to audition talent to cast the show. Good people to get to know. You will meet them first before auditioning for the producers. They are there to weed out the good from the bad and help you if you are so lucky to get to the next level.

choreographer - The person in charge of creating, arranging and teaching the dances or stylized movements.

cold reading - In an audition with casting agents or producers, a cold reading is a new scene that you have never read before. You must be ready to act it out on the spot with no rehearsal. It's tough but impressive, if you are able to deliver the scene right then and there. Yes this is scary, if you don't have the skill set.

Coogan Act - This refers to the trust account where you are required by law to deposit 15% of your child's gross earnings. The money remains in this account until they turn 18. The Coogan account is required in the states of California, New York, Louisiana and New Mexico.

copy - Another word for the script.

craft services - An area on the stage or set where food is set up for the cast and crew. The nosh table is full of food, snacks, drinks and yes, you can get really fat hanging around the cheese puffs and brownies all day. Hint, find the fresh fruit table.

dialogue coach - Your best friend to have on any set. They are in charge of helping you if you forget a line, forget where to stand, or forget what you were supposed to say or do. They are like your second brain. They are right there to feed you the line... we love them! Oh and when you do forget your line all you have to do is yell... "LINE!"

direction - The term that refers to how the director wants you to deliver the line, feel the emotion, and where to move. Basically, what you are told to do is "taking direction."

disfluencies - The pause words that we use that stop the flow of your sentence (um, like, ya know).

dramedy - A TV series that is considered a drama but with levity and humor.

extras - All the people you see in the background of a scene in a movie or TV series. Extras usually do not have lines.

fanbase - These are your loyal fans and followers who buy your music and concert tickets. They follow you on social media and your websites. They watch your TV shows and your movies. These fans are the reason you have a job!

glossophobia - Fear of speaking in public.

improv - When you create or perform music, drama or verse, spontaneously without any preparation and or information of what your scene is about.

industrials - Short films that are produced by a specific company as a tool to promote their brand inside their industry. Industrials are specific to the business they are in and are generally not released to the public.

lip sync - You have recorded a song and are not quite confident that you can sing live on stage. So you pretend you are singing, move your mouth to the recorded track, but nothing comes out of your mouth. You must be very good at this otherwise you will be out of sync with the music. The audience can tell and that is not a good thing. Watch Millie Vanilli... they are the bad version of lip sync.

> **Milli Vanilli - Girl You Know It's True (1990 Grammys)**
>
> http://www.youtube.com/watch?v=cG6fRHzVpNU

lyrics - The words to a song.

manager - The person who is considered the 'marketing director' of your child's career. Managers advise, consult and guide the career of your child. Managers are not necessarily responsible for getting you jobs (see talent agent) but they work with the talent agents as your career marketing director. A manager's commission is generally 10%, although some demand 15% or more.

momagers - The Mom who is also the manager.

monologue - A form of dramatic entertainment, comedic solo or a prolonged speech in a drama by a single actor.

monotone - The continuing sound of a person's voice, that is unchanging in pitch and without intonation.

notes - The notes refer to script revisions the studio, network, writers and director make on the script for you to learn.

on avail - A term used by casting executives to let you know they are very interested in hiring you. In the event that you do get the job, they want to make sure you are available on specific shooting days.

pilot - A one-episode TV show that networks test before green-lighting to a series.

pilot greenlighting - The network has decided to produce the original television script you wrote, one step closer to having it on the air.

pilot season - The time of the year when the many networks are casting for pilots. Generally pilot season for major roles in a series is from February to May plus the month of October. From July through the fall, new shows start production and guest starring roles are cast.

pitch a line - One of the writers involved with the script offers a different joke, a new line to replace the old or a better way to do the scene.

producer's assistant (PA) - The entry level position on a film or TV set. They do just about anything from getting coffee to making copies to running errands. We love our PA's!

protocol - It is the accepted or established code of procedure or behavior in any group; the rules on set. Respect your other actors and crew.

publicist - The publicist or Public Relations Agent's job is to get you press. Press includes TV, radio, magazines, newspapers and all digital media outlets. A good publicist is there to rescue you from bad publicity if, for example, "TMZ" leaks out a horrible story or photo of you not doing something you ever dreamed would be public. Publicists are expensive, and you should only hire one when needed. But, they can cover for you like no other!

running lines - Practicing your lines with someone.

script supervisor - This person is the right hand for the director. They keep track of the script and revisions and provide details about the many takes, the amount of times you act out the scene. The director and the producers need this information to eventually choose the best take to be included in the final edit of the show.

showcase - An event to present talent to the industry. Showcases are usually put on by music and acting schools to present their students for agents and managers. Sometimes talent will organize their own showcase. The purpose of showcases is to seek representation.

sides - The few pages taken out of a script that you receive to read in your audition. Rarely do you get an entire copy of a script.

situation comedy - Usually a 30 minute TV comedy

skill set - An talent's ability

stage direction - The description in the script that tells you how to say the lines or where you are directed to move on a set. It also helps you understand the character.

stage manager - There are two and sometimes three stage managers on a set. The most important one is the 1st Assistant Director (Stage Manager #1) who sets the shoot schedule and works closely with the Director and talent. The 2nd Assistant Director (Stage Manager #2) coordinates the talent to and from the set. At times, there can be a third stage manager when there is a large crowd on that episode or feature film.

stage mom (or dad) - This is what we call moms and dads who cause problems on the set. This is not a compliment. No parent wants to be labeled a stage mom or dad.

stand ins -People who actually replace the cast for lighting, camera blocking, and any rehearsal the camera operators might need. The stand-ins are usually the same height and weight so they resemble the actual actors, who are actually resting in their dressing rooms or if young, in school.

stand on mark - Your mark is where the director tells you to stand and where to look in a particular camera. It is usually marked on the floor with a blue tape about 4 - 5 inches. Cameras are in position to shoot you and if you are not on the mark, you will not be in the shot.

syndication - This is when a series has reached 100 episodes and is then sold as reruns in local markets across the country. This term also refers to a series that is not on a major network and airs directly on stations across the country.

table reading - If you are cast in a series or movie, the table reading is the first day of gathering as a complete cast. You will sit around a 'table', hence a table reading, and all of the cast reads and acts out their parts while seated. This is when the network or film studio hears the script out loud for the first time. Many times they give notes and the script changes because certain scenes did not work when heard out loud. Yes, the script can be a page one rewrite so all new lines are sent to you that night for the next day of rehearsal. Get used to it.

take - The number of times you do the scene over and over - take one, take two and yes take 23! YIKES!

talent agent - The person responsible for 'getting the jobs.' The agent is the talent salesman. Whether or not they are an independent agent or work for a larger agency, they receive a 10% commission that you pay for their services. An agent is a very important person to have in your kid's life.

tone - The kind of attitude the show has or your character has. Is it over the top funny, sincere, sarcastic, jovial or realistic? Usually it's an overall statement of how your character is to be played.

triple threat - An industry term for talent that can sing, act and dance.

vocal coach - A person who works with you on how to use your voice whether you are a singer or an actor. They help you with breathing techniques, vocal power and vocal pace. Vocal coaches teach you how to save your over-used voice, a must for singers and actors.

voice-over - Your recorded voice for a scene where you are heard but not seen. This applies to actors who are using their voices for an animated TV show, movie or commercial.

warm-up - The comic or comedienne that entertains the live audience during the taping of a show. They are there to entertain everyone during set changes, and to keep the audience up to speed on what is happening on stage. Funny, yes they are. Vital, yes they are. They keep the audience invested in the show and more importantly awake!

For additional terminology, check out this dictionary of over 4,000 terms: http://www.amazon.com/dp/0879103639

ACKNOWLEDGMENTS

I would like to thank the following people for their help, advice, knowledge and contribution in completing "Mom! I Want To Be A Star". Writing this book not only took time and effort, but could not have been accomplished without my dedicated business partners, friends and family.

Joanna "JoJo" Lowe, my hard-working sister, was by my side, day and night, from beginning to end in the writing of this book. I never could have written this book without her.

Amber Cordero, a partner of The Dray Way and the book's editor. She structured the book's content and every chapter while keeping us on our writing schedule.

Beth Broday, also a partner of the Dray Way, was the team's cheerleader giving us our daily dose of inspiration to keep going.

To Joel Gotler, our agent from Intellectual Property Group, many thanks for your time and for your belief in The Dray Way. And to PDP, Premier Digital Publishing, thank you for recognizing the value of this book for parents and their kids pursuing their dream.

I would also like to acknowledge my Disney family. Thank you to the cast and crew of "The Suite Life" show franchise and to the network executives for giving me those wonderful years executive producing the longest running show on the Disney Channel!

A huge thank you to all the kid talent I've worked with over the decades. Tia and Tamera Mowry, Tahj Mowry, Dylan and Cole Sprouse, Zac Efron,

Deby Ryan, Miley Cyrus and Selena Gomez. Through your successes and hard work plus the support of your wonderful families, I am able to show parents and future stars that their dream is possible as long as you are prepared to do the work.

And finally, I want to thank my mom, Marge, my brother Barry, his wife Sandra and all my dear friends for their encouragement to pursue this endeavor.

You are all fabulous!

ABOUT THE AUTHOR

Irene Dreayer ("The Dray") is Hollywood's number-one kid-talent expert and trusted career coach for kid talent. She's a thirty-year veteran of family programming, having produced six hundred hours of network TV and discovered some of the biggest kid stars in the business. The Dray is a longtime executive producer for the Disney Channel, the WB, and ABC Family. She executive produced the longest-running show on the Disney Channel, *The Suite Life of Zack & Cody*, as well as *The Suite Life on Deck*, and discovered the shows' stars, Dylan and Cole Sprouse. Dreayer also discovered current Style Network stars Tia and Tamera Mowry as tweens to star in the WB series *Sister, Sister*, which she executive produced for seven seasons. Ms. Dreayer has also produced several TV movies, including the *Suite Life on Deck* movie for the Disney Channel, *Legally Blonde* with Reese Witherspoon for MGM, Disney Channel, and ABC Family, and *Desperately Seeking Santa* for ABC Family.

The Dray Way, founded by Irene Dreayer, is an entertainment career coaching service for kids and a digital community that helps parents and kids navigate their way through show business. Ms. Dreayer works with kids from all over the world via Skype offering guidance, audition coaching, acting, vocal coaching and career consultation for parents. The Dray Way also manages tween talent and is currently developing original content for TV and the web for Tweens and Teens not found on The Disney Channel or Nickelodeon.

The Dray Way Website is an ecommerce site offering private "in person" or Skype consultations with Irene Dreayer for parents and kids across America and worldwide. Visit the website to learn more: http://thedrayway.com.

The Dray Way YouTube Channel is a coaching channel for kids and parents about the ins and outs of the business. Featuring over 50 videos of webinars and Dray's words of wisdom she calls DRAYISMS, The Dray Way Channel is an invaluable source of free useful guidance for kids and parents. http://www.youtube.com/thedrayway

The Dray Way Facebook page is a community of aspiring talented kids and features a weekly contest that allows kids to post video submissions to win the title of "Dray Kid." (http://www.facebook.com/thedrayway) Each week's winner gets a free Skype consultation with The Dray. Winners from The Dray Way weekly Facebook Contest are showcased on our Dray Way Channel. http://www.youtube.com/thedraywaychannel

Open Road Integrated Media is a digital publisher and multimedia content company. Open Road creates connections between authors and their audiences by marketing its ebooks through a new proprietary online platform, which uses premium video content and social media.

Videos, Archival Documents, and New Releases

Sign up for the Open Road Media newsletter and get news delivered straight to your inbox.

Sign up now at
www.openroadmedia.com/newsletters

FIND OUT MORE AT
WWW.OPENROADMEDIA.COM

FOLLOW US:
@openroadmedia and
Facebook.com/OpenRoadMedia

www.ingramcontent.com/pod-product-compliance
Lightning Source LLC
LaVergne TN
LVHW041629070426
835507LV00008B/520